ETHNIC SOVEREIGNTY: AFRICAN NATIONHOOD

Figure 1: **KING YEKUNO AMLAK (1270-1285);** The First Sovereign of the Restored Solomonic Line.

ETHIOPIAN SOVEREIGNTY: AFRICAN NATIONHOOD

Voices from the African Diaspora Call...

Figure 2: The Author Ras E.S.P. Mcpherson (at an ENF/Moa Anbessa & International Working Affiliates led Delegation meeting with The Permanent Mission of the Federal Democratic Republic of Ethiopia (FDRE) to the United Nations, New York, USA, December15th, 1998 launching of the ENF, on the 29th March, 1994, N.Y.., USA).

RAS E.S.P. MCPHERSON

Founder, Chairman of the Ethiopian National Front (ENF);
Founder, Co-Chairman of the Ethiopia Jamaica Society -
New York Chapter (EJSNY); & Co-Chairman of Mo-Anbessa (MOA)
(Jamaica/New York)
THE ETHIOPIAN NATIONAL FRONT (ENF) –
EDUCATION & RESEARCH, ARTS & SCIENCE FOUNDATION

Art & Graphics by **Ras E.S.P. Mc Pherson;**
Cover - Technical Graphics & Layout by **Ras Jason Auguste - "Imperial Ityopian Designs."**

RAS E.S.P. MC PHERSON

Founder, Chairman of the Ethiopian National Front (ENF);
Founder, Co-Chairman of the Ethiopia Jamaica Society -
New York Chapter (EJSNY); & Co-Chairman of Mo-Anbessa (MOA)
(Jamaica/New York)

released 27.5.94; published August, 1999;
republished October 1999

TOWARDS
THE ETHIOPIAN NATIONAL FRONT (ENF) – EDUCATION & RESEARCH,
ARTS & SCIENCE FOUNDATION
"OPEN-HOUSE" BUILDING FUND
WRITE TO:
RAS E.S.P. MC PHERSON
Founder, Chairman
Ethiopian National Front (ENF)
c/o 2507 Holland Avenue
Bronx, New York 10467, USA
PHONE: 718-547-6633; OR: 917-362-5493
E-MAIL: kumina@tbol.net

WEBSITE: http://members.tripod.com/~rastaology

Figure 3: (TheTotem Conquering Lion Seal of MOA ANBESSA i.e. The Conquering Lion Organizing Committee/"Ethiopian for a Constitutiona Monarchy."]

27.5.94/....8.94

TO: The Ethiopian Constitution Commission of The
Transitional Government of Ethiopia; & The Newly
Elected Constituent Assembly
P.O. Box 40812
Addis Ababa
Ethiopia

ETHIOPIAN SOVEREIGNTY: AFRICAN NATIONHOOD:
Voices From The Ethio-Diaspora Call For
A Constitutional Monarchy - Federal Multi-Party Democracy;
Pro-Active Dual Citizenship Rights; The Restitution of The
Land, National Anthem and The Totemic Lion In The National
Flag. A contributing Position Paper from
The ETHIOPIAN NATIONAL FRONT (ENF)
(New York/Jamaica) to
The ETHIOPIAN CONSTITUTION COMMISSION and
newly elected CONSTITUENT ASSEMBLY - of the
Transitional Government of Ethiopia, towards a Draft
Constitution for the creation of a new Ethiopian Constitution.
by Ras E.S.P. Mc Pherson
Founder, Chairman of The Ethiopian National Front (ENF);
Founder, Co-Chairman of The Ethiopia Jamaica Society -
New York Chapter (EJSNY);& Co-Chairman of Mo-
Anbessa (MOA) (Jamaica/New York)

Ethiopian Sovereignty:African Nationhood © 1994, 2000 By E.S.P. Mc Pherson. All rights reserved. No part of this book may be reproduced in any form or by any means including electronic, mechanical or photocopying or stored in a retrieval system without permission in writing from the publisher except by a reviewer who may quote brief passage to be included in a review.

Published by *A&B PUBLISHERS GROUP*, Brooklyn, NY
COVER DESIGN: Ras E.S.P. Mc Pherson
COVER ILLUSTRATION: Ras Jason Auguste "IMPERIAL ITYOPIAN DESIGNS."

Library of Congress Cataloging-In-Publication Data

McPherson, E.S.P. (Everton S. P.)
Ethiopian sovereignty: African nationhood / E.S.P. McPherson.
  p. cm.
Includes bibliographical references (p.) and index.
  ISBN 1-886433-32-1
1. Ethiopian—History—20th century. 2. Ethiopian National Front.
3. Ethiopians—United States—Political activity.   4. Political refugees—Ethiopia—Political activity.6. Rastafari movement—Political aspects. I. Title: Ethiopian sovereignty: African nationhood. II. Title
DT386   .M38 2000
320.963—dc21   00-060596

Printed in Canada

Author's Website: http://members.tripod.com/~rastaology
Author's E-mail: kumina@tbol.net Phone: 917-362-5493
"ORDER OF THE PRECEPTS"/
Ethio-Rastaology Educational Program, No.1

TOWARDS
THE ETHIOPIAN NATIONAL FRONT (ENF) –
EDUCATION & RESEARCH,
ARTS & SCIENCE FOUNDATION
"OPEN-HOUSE" BUILDING FUND
WRITE TO:
RAS E.S.P. MC PHERSON
Founder, Chairman
Ethiopian National Front (ENF)
c/o 2507 Holland Avenue

CONTENTS

Opening Prayer/Ethiopic Masonic Chant 3
THE ENF 4
GENESIS TO ENF'S POSITION PAPER 8
ETHIOPIAN SOVEREIGNTY BY BIRTH/BLOOD: SELF DETERMINATION 21
AFRICAN NATIONHOOD: A UNION OF SOVEREIGN STATES 28
CONSTITUTIONAL MONARCHY / CEREMONIAL FEDERALISM 40
MULTI-PARTY DEMOCRACY: ETHIO-DIASPORA ELECTORAL INVOLVEMENT 47
ACTIVE DUAL CITIZENSHIP RIGHTS: ELECTED BY BIRTH/BLOOD 55
THE ERITREAN SECESSIONIST ACT & DUAL CITIZENSHIP 64
THE REINSTITUTION OF THE LAND: REPATRIATION WITH REPARATION KEY 64
RETURN OF THE NATIONAL ANTHEM AND THE TOTEMIC LION FLAG: ROYALTY, BRAVERY & COURAGE 76
CONCERNS: 79
RESOLUTIONS: LEAP OF WISDOM / CONSCIOUS EVOLUTION 85
Charge: 85
Bibliography 88
ETHIOPIAN NATIONAL FRONT - (ENF EDUCATION & RESEARCH, ARTS & SCIENCE FOUNDATION CATALOGUE 102
Forthcoming Publications 103
RAS E.S.P. MC PHERSON PUBLISHED & DISTRIBUTED BY A&B PUBLISHERS GROUP 105
INDEX 106

PHOTO CREDITS INFO.:

ENF *Seal [-representing original Front Cover of original Paper presented to the Transitional* Government of Ethiopia newly elected Constituent Assembly.]

Figure 1: KING YEKUNO AMLAK (1270-1285); The First Sovereign of the Restored Solomonic Line. (From a late eighteenth century MA., British Museum Orient 503.) Richard Pankhurst B. Sc. (Econ), Ph.D, An Introduction to The Economic History of Ethiopia from easrly times to 1800, (LALIBELA HOUSE), 1961, [p. 47]. ii

Figure 2: The Author; (at an ENF/Moa Anbessa & International Working Affiliates led Delegation meeting with The Permanent Mission of the Federal Democratic Republic of Ethiopia (FDRE) to the United Nations, New York, USA, December15th, 1998 launching of the ENF, on the 29th March, 1994, N.Y.., USA). iii

Figure 3: (TheTotem Conquering Lion Seal of MOA ANBESSA i.e. The Conquering Lion Organizing Committee/ "Ethiopian for a Constitutional Monarchy."] iv

Figure 4: H.I.M. v

Figure 5: **r-l**: Ras E.S.P. Mc Pherson (EJSNY Co-Chair/MOA Co-Chair, at the launching of the **Ethiopian National Front/ENF**, through a presentation entitled: **"MAKE MAN -BLOW BREATH - GIVE LIFE - WAKE UP THE NATION RESURRECTION FROM `THE VALLEY OF DRY BONES' -YES IT IS THAT TIME!,"** 29th March 1994: Sis Gem Morrison (Sect of the EWF Inc.,) *(Photo: Ras Makalini, EJS Press & Publication Committee member)* 7

Figure 6: [center] Bro. Nakim A. Bey (Amb. of the Moorish Council of Nat. & Int. Affairs); [left] Dr. Rev. J. Johnstone (Founder Chair of the Ethiopian Diaspora Movement, Inc.); [right] Ras Firm Selassie (Nyahbinghi Order Rep.) *(Photo: Ras Makalini, EJS Press and Publication Committee member)* 9

Figure 7: r-l: Ras Enoch (Deeperlite Spiritual & Cultural Liberation Theological Assembly); Ras Mora (EWF, Inc, Exec.); Ras Mc Pherson (center) listens as Ras Firm submits his greetings and questions. *(Photo: Ras Makalini, EJS Press and Publication Committee member)* 9

Figure 8: left-right: [partly hidden] Ras Firm Selassie (Nyahbinghi Order Rep.); [standing] Ras Adoniyas Haile Eyasus I (Lion of Judah Society/Embassy); [seated] Ras E.S.P. Mc Pherson (EJSNY Co-Chair/MOA Co-Chair); Bro. Nakim A. Bey (Amb. Of the Moorish Council); Sis. Damalia (EJSNY/MOA Member); Sis. Bev. (Rep. & Sect. of the Iniversal Rastafari Inity/IRI); Bro. .. (Moorish Council Exec.); Ras Berhane Maskal (EJSNY Co-Chair/MOA Exec.); Bro. Rev. Dr. J. J. Johnstone (the Ethiopian Diaspora Movement, Inc.); Sis. ... (EWF, Inc. Exec.) *(Photo: Ras Makalini, EJS Press and Publication Committee member)*..10

Figure 9: [center] Ras Firm (Nyahbinghi Order Rep.) officially submits his greetings and questions, in the aftermath of Ras Mc Pherson (EJSNY/MOA) presentation (and each formation – respectively); [left] while EWF, Executive, Sis. .... listens intently; [right] a and EWF, Inc. Sect./Exec. take *Records*/minutes of this historic gathering. *(Photo: Ras Makalini, EJS Press and Publication Committee member)*.......11

Figure 10: l-r: *Ras Amlak/Jerome Martinez - President of the EWF, Inc. - Host of the EWF, Inc. Executive meeting called that led to the formation of the ENF; Ras Mora - an Executive of the EWF, Inc.; 29th March, 1994. (Photo: Ras Makalini, EJS Press and Publication Committee member)* 15

Figure 11: Ras Mc Pherson [seated - 4th left] is thanked by Ras Amlak, the EWF, Inc. Local No. 1 President, for calling the historic meeting. (Photo: Ras Makalini, EJS Press and Publication Committee member)...17

Figure 12: (The late) The Rt. Hon. Prof. Asrat Woldeyes [Prisoner of Conscience] See "Yes, Ethiopia is a colony of Eritreal," Moresh Vol. 4, No. 4/5, 1996 (Ethiopian Amhara Organization; Moresh, P.O. Box 6446, Minneapolis), MN 55406, September, 1996..18

Figure 13: *H. I. M.* newly created Government, June, 1931, implied *He was the first Monarch* to democratize *His Throne*: Rastalogically, *Theocracy came to Earth.*..23

Figure 14: The Rt. Hon. President General Marcus Garvey [second from right] reviewing a UNIA & ACL parade, in the 1922. 23

Figure 15: The Rt. Hon. *Saint* Marcus Mosiah Garvey, D.C.L/ Dr. of Civil Law; & D.D./Dr. of Divinity..24

Figure 16: H.I.M. delivering the opening speech at the African Heads of State and Governments, Summit Conference, that led to the formation of the Organization of African Unity (O.A.U.), in Africa Hall, Addis Ababa, Ethiopia, May 23, 1963. 29

Figure 17: [r.-l.] *H. I. M.* and the late former Crown Prince of Ethiopia, H.I.H. Merd Azmatch Asfa Wossen Haile Selassie [; who was later elevated to: H.I.M. Amha Selassie I, Conquering Lion of the Tribe of Judah, Emperor of Ethiopia.] 34

Figure 18: [l.-r.] H. I. M. and H.I.H. Merd Azmatch Asfa Wossen Haile Selassie. 35

Figure 19: [r-l] [The late – and former] Crown Prince Asfa Wossen, and [then] Princess Medferiash Worq – his wife [who was later elevated and renamed – H. I. M. Medferiash Worq Abede]......35

Figure 20: [l-r] Princess Sifrash, Princess Mariam-Sena, H.I.M. Medferiash Worq Abede, H.I.H. Crown-Prince-Designate Zera Yacob, Princess Sihin, and H.I.M. Amha Selassie with his grand daughter, Ida. 36

Figure 21: The late - H.I.H. Merd Azmatch Asfa Wossen Haile Selassie:/ H.I.M. Amha Selassie 36

Figure 22: His Imperial Highness Prince Ermias Sahle-Selassie Haile-Selassie, Grandson of HIM Emperor Haile Selassie I, and currently President of the Crown Council of Ethiopia, 1993. ...37

Figure 23: His Imperial Highness Prince Bekere Fikre-Selassie, Grandson of HIM Emperor Amha Selassie I, and currently Viceroy (Enderassé) of the Crown Council of Ethiopia, 1993 37

Figure 24: H.I.H. Zere Yacob. 38

Figure 25: H.I.H. Zere Yacob, Crown Prince of Ethiopia 38

Figure 26: THE CROWN & THE THRONE: [r.-l.] H. R H. Prince Bekere Fikre-Selassie - Enderasse and Viceroy of The Crown Council of Ethiopia is greeted by Ras E.S.P. Mc Pherson - ENF Founder Chair/MOA Co-Chair (USA/Ja.)/ EJSNY Founder Co-Chair, at an Audience *given by The Crown Council of Ethiopia to the ENF/MOA (USA/Ja.)/EJSNY*, held in the Bronx, New York, USA, on the 29th of January, 1998; between 3.40 p. m.-6.45 p. m. At this historic meeting the ENF/EJSNY/ MOA (USA/Ja.) presented a working "PRO-ACTIVE AGENDA," entitled, "THE WATCHERS FROM WITHIN: THE THRONE & THE CROWN." Here also, the ENF Continental & Diaspora PRO-ACTIVE SOVEREIGN CONSTITUTIONAL AGENDA, entitled:

"...World Leaders, what about Ethiopia?," was ratified by *The Crown* 39

Figure 27: ENF/MOA/EJSNY AUDIENCE WITH THE CROWN: [l-r] Rases Claude, Mc Pherson, Dave; Sis. Amma; H.R.H. Prince Bekere Fikre-Selassie – *Enderasse* and *Viceroy of The Crown Council of Ethiopia*; Rases Bunny, Robert/Negus. (29/1/98.) 39

Figure 28: Ras Martimo Planno - one of the earliest Rastafari Intellectual and Pan-Africanist of the mid 1950s to late 1960s. 53

Figure 29: UPON H. I. M. VISIT TO JA.: "Arrival – Adoring Crowds Breaks Protocol [April 21, 1966]." 60

Figure 30: STATE VISIT OF H. I. M. HAILE SELASSIE TO JAMAICA: Pictured at King's House are His Imperial Majesty Haile Selassie I - Emperor of The Kingdom of Ethiopia (3rd from Right); His Excellency Sir Clifford, G.C.M.G., G.C.V.D. - Governor General of Jamaica representing The Queen of Jamaica (2nd from Right). Others are (L-R-R) Her Royal Highness Imebet Sofiya Desta - Granddaughter of H. I. M.; Her Excellency Lady Campbell (Wife of The Governor-General); Mrs. E. Kean - Lady-in-Waiting to Her Excellency Lady Campbell and daughter of Sir Clifford and Lady Campbell; and His Highness Prince Mikael - Grandson of His Imperial Majesty 61

Figure 31: HAPPY CRUSH: The pressures of the masses were terrific everywhere. 'COURIER' Cameraman got this crush-squeezing shot of His Imperial Majesty followed by Governor-General Sir Clifford Campbell and a very protective Brigadier General Assefa Demise, Principal Aide-de-Camp to His Imperial Majesty 62

Figure 32: AT OFFICIAL CEREMONY: In the Royal Box His Imperial Majesty heard Welcoming Addresses and fittingly replied. H. I. M. pictured in the course of His reply 63

Figure 33: Members of the Jamaican Back to Africa delegation with President Dr. Kwame Nkrumah, Accra Ghana, 1961; *standing* l-r: Munroe Scarlett, Mr. Victor Reid; Dr. Leslie; President Nkrumah; Bro. Douglas Mack; Bro. Martimo Planno, Hon. E. H. Lake, Minister of Social Welfare, Antigua; Bro. Philmore Alvaranga; and Ghanaian Protocol Chief; *sitting l-r:* Mr. Blackwood, the U. N. I. A. & A. C. L. Delegate; and Mr. Cecil Gordon, E. W. F., Inc. Rep. 67

Figure 34: [left] Nii Amo Nakwah II, the Obtobulum Mensah, Paramount Chief of the Ashanti praying for members of the Jamaican Back to Africa Delegation, in Accra Ghana 1961; Bro. Douglas Mack [center] 69

Figure 35: "Purification of stools and skins ceremony in Jamestown Accra (Dec '95) – Jah Blue & Ras Binghi." 69

Figure 36: "The Land in Akwamu, given to black people of the diaspora – Ras Binghi & Jah Blue with Chiefs and Queen Mother." 70

Figure 37: Professor Asrat Woldeyes permitted to seek medical attention abroad. 82

Figure 38: "Haile Selassie I" [Salutes.]...86

Figure 39: Afewerk Tekle, Ethiopia's leading artist [mural of H. I. M.] 86

Figure 40: [H. I. M. (Right) Honors the late Great Chief Warrior & Elder Statesman - President Jomo Kenyatta (Left) of Kenya.].87

ETHIOPIAN SOVEREIGNTY:
AFRICAN NATIONHOOD
Voices from the African Diaspora Call...

(E.N.F.)

Ras E.S.P. McPherson

Publishers Group
Brooklyn, NY 11238

"...Ethiopia Is Guarded Without: Let Ethiopia Be Guarded Within.... Ethiopians Who Are Present Among Us Are More Especially **'The Watchers From Within.'"**

Honorable members of the Electoral Commission of the Transitional Government of Ethiopia, and recently elected members of the Constituent Assembly - and respective constituencies, We bring you fraternal Greetings from the Ethiopian National Front (ENF) executives and respective constituencies on the ground in the struggle; in particular from the Ethiopia Jamaica Society (EJS) - and EJS New York Chapter and Our international affiliates, as Mo-Anbessa (The Conquering Lion Organizing Committee) (Jamaica/New York) executives.

Together, We are the concerned Voices of the Ethio-Diaspora formations, calling for the Liberation of Ethiopia - and Africa. WE are Your long lost and NOW found Brothers and Sisters: **NATION,** crying, pleading and actively working towards the reclaiming of Our Ethiopian Sovereignty and African Nationhood: the establishment of **A SINGLE AFRICAN GOVERNMENT**. As the Scriptures did (pre-) RECORD: *"By the rivers of Babylon, there we sat down, yea, we wept, when we remembered Zion [ETHIOPIA/AFRICA] ...."* (Psalm 137 verse 1.) [1]

We, are - in the main – *"the prodigal Sons and Daughters"* / indigent one's who, having experienced the World through the gross genocidal rape of Our Continent and Nation-at-large, who need, and DEMAND, NOW, to come home! (St. Luke 15 verses 11-32.) [2]

---

[1] See **The Bible,** (King James Version).
[2] See **The Bible,** (King James Version).

THE ENF

THE ETHIOPIAN NATIONAL FRONT came into being on Tuesday the 29th of March 1994 at an extra-ordinary meeting that was called by the EJS New York Chapter, that was held at the Head Quarters of the Ethiopian World Federation - His Imperial Majesty Local No. 1, situated in Brooklyn, New York. The ENF [Inc.] is a democratic coalition of Ethio-Jamaicans, Ethio-Americans and the Rastafari International Community Social Movements, Communal Enterprises and Black Fraternities.

Ideologically, We are **"Royalists"** and **"Pan Ethio-cultural internationalists,"** who have rightly and timely come together as a organic Front, as partners in solidarity with Ethiopia and Ethiopians in her quest for Sovereignty through *"a renewed constitution,"* by way of an executive fiat - *"constitutional law."* For Us, the recognition, process, adherence and application of **"the rule of law"** transcends human and ideological diversities, and thus provides the natural basis for Us to UNITE: to see and pro-actively work towards the unification of Ethiopia (and Africa).

The present constitutional exercise of the Transitional Government of Ethiopia (TGE) Constituent Assembly, that is slated to lead to the creation of a new "Constitutional Draft," which is to be voted upon in September/October of 1994, presents an opportunity for the concerned scattered/ exiled Ethiodiaspora to create and take affirmative actions, in the spirit of *a "unity of purpose"*, to serve the common good of Ethiopia and all Ethiopians: Africans.

As such the adapted motto of the ENF is **"SOVEREIGNTY & NATIONHOOD; UNITY IN DIVERSITY: ETHIOPIA FOR ETHIOPIANS, THOSE AT HOME AND THOSE ABROAD."**

As "Royalist" We will relentlessly see to **The Restoration of the Solomonic Dynasty -in the form of A "Constitutional Monarchy."** This was set out in **the "LAWS OF SUCCESSION"** of the June 16th 1931 Constitution given by His Imperial Majesty Haile Selassie I to Ethiopia, that was respectfully revised in 1955, and August of 1974 in the form a **"Draft Constitution"**;[3] and has continually been enunciated by the exiled and legitimate Crown Council of Ethiopia, and H.I.H. Amha Selassie I - for example in **"The Message"/"Holy Declaration"** of April 6th 1988; and has been furthered by the establishment of, and **"Civil Guardian"** role and works of Mo-Anbessa - internationally, since June 29th 1991.

As Pan-Ethiopianist, We are contending that the success of a Federal Multi-Party Democracy in Ethiopia represents the perquisite and preamble of a needed Federal arrangement of African States - respectively, that will bring into being Our ultimate: **A SINGLE AFRICAN GOVERNMENT** - even as set out by the Organization of African Unity (OAU) historic and culturally significant Paper: **"AFRICA 2000 A Continental Government for Africa."**

The most immediate affirmative collective action of the respective Heads of States on the Continent and throughout the diaspora towards such a realization, rests within the legal sovereign constitutional empowerment that **"dual citizenship"** will give to Our Nation, when comprehensively implemented. This represents a corner stone of Our Paper's position, as We collectively call for the constitutional entrenchment of **the**

---

[3] See His Imperial Majesty's radio broadcast, on the 5th of March 1974, calling for a "Draft Constitution," speech, dubbed: **"A GOVERNMENT DECLARATION OF GUIDANCE,"** stated among other things: "We have issued intentions that the Constitution should be reviewed **in accordance with the needs of Our People and in the new spirit of unity**." [my emphases.] It can be found in E.S.P. Mc Pherson, **RASTAFARI and POLITICS: Sixty Years of a Developing Cultural Ideology. A Sociology of Development Perspective**, (Black International Iyahbinghi Press, Frankfield, Clarendon, Jamaica), September 2nd 1991, pp. 55-59.

Ethio-diaspora active participation in the civil life of Ethiopia, e.g. in future electoral exercises.

This position also leads Us to another cornerstone of Our Paper: the need for the **RECLAIMING of THE LAND/Africa; the REINSTITUTION/ RESTITUTION OF LAND IN ETHIOPIA** by respective constituencies of the Ethio-diaspora.

The ENF represented constituencies are **"non-aligned"** - practitioners of **"cooperative democracy."** We work from a position of consensus, and aim to share with Ethiopia/ Ethiopians (Africans) this working affirmative position and alternative development strategizing method.[4] It is one which calls upon Us to submerge Our differences/unique divergences, and work with Our overwhelming commonalties. Such represents a notably paradigm-shift, that Ethiopia has been devoid of in the last twenty-two (22) years, that **must** be naturally presented by the Ethio-diaspora to Our Peoples on the Continent. Our complete commitment to this peaceful, just and democratic participating development path has thus led Our organized and trained intelligent cadre of thinkers to present this Position Paper. It represents A CALL FOR (INTER-) NATIONAL RECONCILIATION.

---

[4] See "What we seek for Africa The Words of His Imperial Majesty Haile Selassie of Ethiopia," **Reggae & Africa Beat**, Vol. 8 #1 1989, p. 7; ibid, Mc Pherson, **RASTAFARI...**, p. 2.

Figure 5: TOP & BOTTOM PHOTOS: **r-l**: Ras E.S.P. Mc Pherson (EJSNY Co-Chair/MOA Co-Chair, at the launching of the **Ethiopian National Front/ENF**, through a presentation entitled: **"MAKE MAN -BLOW BREATH - GIVE LIFE - WAKE UP THE NATION RESURRECTION FROM 'THE VALLEY OF DRY BONES' -YES IT IS THAT TIME!,"** 29th March 1994: Sis Gem Morrison (Sect of the EWF Inc.,)

GENESIS TO ENF'S POSITION PAPER

IT IS NOTEWORTHY TO INFORM Your Honorably members that respective ENF constituencies have always expressed a continued constitutional concern. It remains the basis of the respective trajectories paths of the ENF members procedural and daily socio-cultural activities. For example the active involvement and contributions made by one of Our ENF member: **the Jamaica Chapter of the Jamaica Progressive League**, in the local constitutional reform exercise that took place in 1991, and is yet to be completed. (The implications of this alternative Constitution presented by the JPL will be later discussed in this Paper.) The constitutional challenges and **EATUP Manifesto** presentation by **the Royal Ethiopian Judah Coptic Church**, a neo-traditional wing of the Ancient Nyahbinghi Order of His Majesty Haile Selassie I - Rastafari community, and a Founding member of the EJS/Moa-Anbessa Steering Committee, is another example of this constitutional consciousness, and due respect for "the rule of law." Here in the New York, USA ENF constituencies as **the EWF Local No. 1, The Haile Selassie Theocracy Governmant of His Majesty Haile Selassie I, the JPL,** and **the Deeperlite Spiritual and Cultural Liberation Theological Assembly Movement**, remain constitutional correct in their respective positions. In particular, ENF's member, **the Moorish Council of National and International Affairs** sovereign based premise that is rooted in their just interpretation of "the rule of law," has empowered them with the rights of "dual citizenship" within the Meso-American Iberian bloc. This constitutional franchise of **the Moors** is further seen in their won rights of "diplomatic immunity," that is inclusive of the rights to travel without a passport within these spheres, and to carry a firearm, among other things.

Figure 6:TOP PHOTO: **[center]** Bro. Nakim A. Bey (Amb. of the Moorish Council of Nat. & Int. Affairs); **[left]** Dr. Rev. J. Johnstone (Founder Chair of the Ethiopian Diaspora Movement, Inc.); **[right]** Ras Firm Selassie (Nyahbinghi Order Rep.)

Figure 7: BOTTOM PHOTO : r-l: Ras Enoch (Deeperlite Spiritual & Cultural Liberation Theological Assembly); Ras Mora (EWF, Inc, Exec.); Ras Mc Pherson (center) listens as Ras Firm submits his greetings and questions.

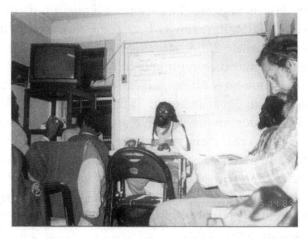

Figure 8: left-right: [partly hidden] Ras Firm Selassie (Nyahbinghi Order Rep.); [standing] Ras Adoniyas Haile Eyasus I (Lion of Judah Society/Embassy); [seated] Ras E.S.P. Mc Pherson (EJSNY Co-Chair/MOA Co-Chair); Bro. Nakim A. Bey (Amb. Of the Moorish Council); Sis. Damalia (EJSNY/MOA Member); Sis. Bev. (Rep. & Sect. of the Iniversal Rastafari Inity/IRI); Bro. .. (Moorish Council Exec.); Ras Berhane Maskal (EJSNY Co-Chair/MOA Exec.); Bro. Rev. Dr. J. J. Johnstone (the Ethiopian Diaspora Movement, Inc.); Sis. ... (EWF, Inc. Exec.)

Noteworthy also, is the recognition by the Jamaican Rastafari Community of the legitimate rights of the Crown Council of Ethiopia, in exile since 1974. Resulting from the historic second National Rastafari Convention held on November 17th 18th of 1991, at the Student Union, University of the West Indies, Mona Campus, Kingston, Jamaica. There was a **SUMMARY RESOLUTION** recognition of the legitimacy of the quest for the Restoration/ **Acknowledgement** of the Solomonic Dynasty, in the form of a "Constitutional Monarchy."[5]

---

[5] See Ilect of Throne: Ras Everton Mc Pherson; Ilect of Records: Jasper Fertuado/Ras Ivi; Ilect of Treasury: Ras Irie Lion, **"A Summary Report of the National Rastafari Assembly Hosted by the Nyahbinghi Order of His Majesty Rastafari, held at the Social Welfare Centre of the University of the West Indies, Mona, Kingston, Jamaica, Saturday November 17th-Sunday 18th, 1990.,"** (The Nyahbinghi Order of His Majesty Rastafari International Coordinating Working Committee) [RICWC], c/o Ras Boanerges, Gold Smith

Figure 9: [center] Ras Firm (Nyahbinghi Order Rep.) officially submits his greetings and questions, in the aftermath of Ras Mc Pherson (EJSNY/MOA) presentation (and each formation – respectively); [left] while EWF, Executive, Sis. .... listens intently; [right] a and EWF, Inc. Sect./Exec. take *Records*/minutes of this historic gathering.

Also more noteworthy of this recognition, was the immediate activation of The Royal Family of Ethiopia's declared Restoration Programme, that was immediately embraced by the newly formed **EJS**, on **Sunday the 22nd of December, 1991,**[6] **in Gordon Town, St. Andrew, Jamaica**. Which, is now made further manifest in the **EJS** initiated and led activities, that has led to this other historic presentation, to be now chronologically outlined:

Villa, Lot 215, Mona P.O., Kingston) November 1990, pp. 1-2; also in ibid, Mc Pherson, **RASTAFARI and POLITICS..**, pp. 198-199.

[6] See **"ETHIOPIA JAMAICA SOCIETY FORMED PRESS RELEASE,"** December 23, 1991; **EJS Newsletter**, Vol. 1 No. 1 Feb.-Mar., 1992, pp. 3; see also "New Rastafarian group formed," **The Jamaica Record** (News), December 28th, 1991; see also "Formation of Ethiopia-Jamaica [Society] Association," **The Weekend Star** (Positive Vibes), December 27, 1991, p. 4.

- On **Saturday March 19, 1994** the EJS/Moa-Anbessa Co-Chairman, Ras Everton Mc Pherson was invited by the Ethiopian Patriotic Organizations - affiliates of the EJS, to participate in a demonstration against the EPRDF/TGE undemocratic, illegal, atrocious continued activities; and various policy steps made, and now been taken towards the drafting of a new constitution. Here a Paper entitled: **"ETHIOPIA: ONE NATION - MANY PEOPLES: EJS & MO-ANBESSA decries the TGE/EPRDF (TPLF [MLL]/EPLF) regime; THE DIASPORA CALLS FOR A 'REAL DEMOCRATIC CONSTITUENT ASSEMBLY,' CREATED CONSTITUTION & A PROGRAM-OF-ACTION."**

Here, the major point put forth was that: with the present ongoing constitutional exercises afoot, represented a 360 degree turn within the political history of Ethiopia, that was made necessary with the illegal overthrow of the Monarchial system of Government in 1974, and the later overthrow of the communist regime of the Dergue in 1991. Thus, the only "LEGAL" constitutional and correct basis upon which, to proceed was to recognize the legality and obvious merits of the **"Draft Constitution"** of August 1974. The objectives of this **"Draft Constitution"** of 1974 ordered by His Imperial Majesty, are best set out in his 5th of March 1974 nationwide broadcast, entitled: **"A GOVERNMENT DECLARATION OF GUIDANCE:"** "We have issued intentions that the Constitution should be reviewed in accordance with the needs of Our People and in the new spirit of unity..."

- Also on **Saturday March 19th**, at Columbia University, Ras Everton Mc Pherson - as Co-Chair of the EJS and on behalf of the EJS N.Y. Chapter, and as Ilect of Throne of The Nyahbinghi Order of His Majesty Rastafari International Coordinating Working Committee (RICWC), made an invaluable contribution to the TGE's Electoral Committee exercise that was carried out by the TGE's Permanent Mission to the United Nations, at Columbia University, New York, United States.

The areas and issues focused and voted upon were those dealing with the questions surrounding "dual citizenship;" a "Constitutional Monarchy"/ "Parliamentary System" (which We explained to all gathered is one and the same - as set out by the August 1974 **"Constitutional Draft," "The Message.."/ "HOLY DECLARATION,"**[7] and numerous Mo-Anbessa literate and oral sources). Also dealt with was the illegal secessionist act of Eritrea - whose representatives/cohorts were ridiculously calling for 'dual citizenship.'

Mr. Teruneh Zenna, the TGE's Economic Counsellor at the U.N. Permanent Mission, invited Ras Mc Pherson - twice - to put in writing Our expressed positions, and forward it to the Mission, who will then dispatch it to the Electoral Commission in Ethiopia. This was firstly said to the EJS/Moa-Anbessa Chair in a formal interview with the Mr. Zenna, at the first in-

---

[7] Ibid, **"EXCERPTS FROM THE CO-CHAIRMAN OF THE EJS & MO-ANBESSA, & ILECT OF THRONE OF THE NYAHBINGHI ORDER OF HIS MAJESTY RASTAFARI INTERNATIONAL COORDINATING WORKING COMMITTEE,"** (Saturday 14th March 1994); also see ibid, **"(THE ETHIOPIA JAMAICA SOCIETY LED) MEETING BETWEEN THE ETHIOPIAN NATIONAL FRONT AND THE DEPUTY AMBASSADOR, MR. FIFFHA, OF THE PERMANENT MISSION OF ETHIOPIA TO THE UNITED NATIONS, ON THE 11TH OF APRIL, 1994, AT 866 UN PLAZA, NEW YORK, U.S.A. THE QUEST OF ETHIOPIAN SOVEREIGNTY: AFRICAN NATIONHOOD AGENDA"** (attachment), p. 9: ."...It is Our view that - because of the role of 'The Monarchy' throughout Ethiopia's history, that the role that Amha Selassie [I] as **"The Constitutional Monarchy"** could play in Ethiopia - would be a very **"Symbolic"** one in unifying Ethiopia.

Secondly, in 1974 August there was a "Draft Constitution " that was put through in Parliament. And the provisions of that Constitution gave way for the power would lay in the Parliament - the locus of power would remain in the Parliament, but there would be a "Constitution Monarchy." That means that provision were already been made by His Majesty to devolve power to The People.

And because of this I am saying "47" [The Constitutional Monarchy] and "48" [The Parliamentary System], for Us the Rastafari Community represent one and the same.

Ahm, if you read **"The Message ...,"** that was given by His Majesty Amha Selassie [1]. It outlines the workings of this "Constitutional Monarchy" with the locus been in Parliament. And that coupled with the "Draft Constitution" of 1974 give Us an incline as to how this could operate..." [see attachment.]

termission given; and secondly, reiterated by Mr. Zenna himself from the podium, where he was one of the active convening Chairman of this constitutional exercise. Mr. Zenna was especially positively interested in the legitimate rights of the "dual citizenship" quest of the diaspora.

- On **Tuesday March 29th 1994** the ENF was formed. The ENF consist of **the Iniversal Rastafari Inity, the Ethiopian Diaspora Movement, Inc., the Jamaica Progressive League - N.Y. Chapter, the Nyahbinghi Order of His Majesty Haile Selassie I Theocracy Governmant, the Moorish Council of National and International Affairs, The Deeperlite Spiritual and Cultural Liberation Theological Assembly, the Lion of Judah Society and EWF Inc. Local No. 1**.

Figure 10: l-r: *Ras Amlak/Jerome Martinez - President of the EWF, Inc. - Host of the EWF, Inc. Executive meeting called that led to the formation of the ENF; Ras Mora - an Executive of the EWF, Inc.; 29ᵗʰ March, 1994..*

(Please note that the majority of these Movements are regional and international in their membership/executive authority).

There was a resounding resolve to focus Our attention and activities on the civil development of Ethiopia, with a view of becoming further positively involved in the present constitutional exercises in Ethiopia. As such, it was decided that a ENF delegation would accompany the EJS N.Y. Chapter to the TGE Permanent Mission to the UN offices to see His Excellency Dr. Mulgeta Etewea, the Ambassador of the TGE.

- On **Wednesday March 30ᵗʰ 1994**, EJS Co-Chair and newly appointed ENF Chairman reported the birth of the ENF and Our wish to visit the TGE UN Mission as a collective. The EJS invitation, now became extended to the ENF delegation.

- A Paper dated: **4.4.94**, written by Ras Everton/E.S.P. Mc Pherson, EJS/Moa-Anbessa Co-Chairman, Chairman of the Pan Africanist Movement Constitutional Committee (Jamaica), Negusa Nagast (King of Kings)/Deputy Grand Master) of the Queen of Sheba and Pharaohs Masonic Movement, and endorsed by the ENF was sent to the 7th Pan Africanist Congress, held in Kampala, Uganda. The Paper is entitled: **"ETHIOPIANISM-OF-OLD, PAN-AFRICANISM, MODERN ETHIOPIANISM, AND RASTAFARI: TOWARDS PAN-ETHIOPIANIZATION (SOVE-REIGNTY) AND A SINGLE CONTINENTAL GOVERNMENT (NATIONHOOD)."**

- On **April 11th 1994**, led by the EJS N.Y. Chapter, a five man delegation was introduced by Mr. Teruneh Zenna. We met with His Excellency Mr. Fiffha, the Deputy Ambassador (who sat in for Mr. Etewea who was unavoidable absent and accordingly sent his greetings and apologies). Present were: Ras Everton, Co-Chairman of EJS/Moa-Anbessa, Chairman of the ENF; Ras Berhane Maskal, Chairman EJS New York Chapter; Ras Makalini, a EJS Press and Publication Committee member; Bro. Rev. J. Johnson, Founder-Chairman of the Ethiopian Diaspora Movement, Inc.; Ras Ameyn Ras Adoniyas Haile Eyasu I, Founder-Chairman of the Lion of Judah Society A Paper/Agenda entitled: **"(THE ETHIOPIA JAMAICA SOCIETY - NEW YORK CHAPTER) LED MEETING BETWEEN THE ETHIOPIAN NATIONAL FRONT AND THE DEPUTY AMBASSADOR, MR. FIFFHA, OF THE PERMANENT MISSION OF ETHIOPIA TO THE UNITED NATIONS, ON THE 11th OF APRIL, 1994, AT 866 UN PLAZA, NEW YORK, U.S.A. THE QUEST OF ETHIOPIAN SOVEREIGNTY: AFRICAN NATIONHOOD AGENDA"**

- On May 19th 1994, an English translation of the Constituency Assembly proposal was sent to the EJS International H.Q./ENF H.Q.. Chairman Ras Mc Pherson again met with Bro. Teruneh Zenna, the Economic Counsellor; and with the Deputy Ambassador, Mr. Fiffha.

Entitled: **"The Transitional Government of Ethiopia The Constitution Commission A Paper on Basic Constitutional Concepts presented for Public Discussion November 1993 Addis Ababa."** This while helpful, was not the translation requested. We wanted to receive along with this Paper, the exact one used at the Columbia University Constitutional exercise, that presented options on the various areas of this proposed Constitutional Draft, that We had discussed and voted upon.

- On August 17th Ras Mc Pherson, as ENF Chairman received from Mr. Teruneh Zenna, of the TGE's U.N. Permanent Mission Economic Counsellor, a copy of the June 5th Constituent Assembly Election results written in Amharic), along with a document entitled: **"ELECTION NEWS,"** indicating provisional results in a **"..TABLE OF RESULTS"** for Regions 14 and 13 (written in English).[8] While outlining how the EPRDF had won almost all of these contested seats, this document pointed to the many (internationally) observed irregularities throughout this electoral exercise (which We will elaborate on in Our subsection on **"CONCERNS"**).

We questioned and formally interviewed Mr. Fiffha about:

i) the historic and massive demonstrations by an array of Ethiopian formation in Washington, upon the visit of the TGE's President Meles Zenawi, first visit to the U.S.A., on August 11th;[9]

Figure 11: Ras Mc Pherson [seated – 4th left] is thanked by Ras Amlak, the EWF, Inc. Local No. 1 President, for calling the historic meeting.

---

[8] (Received June 1994).

[9] See for example **"URGENT CALL TO SAVE ETHIOPIA FROM DISINTEGRATION AND ETHNIC DICTATORSHIP! YESTERDAY YUGOSLAVIA AND SOMALIA, TODAY IT IS RWANDA, AND TOMORROW IT MIGHT BE OUR OWN ETHIOPIA!,"** (A Paper put out by The Coordinating Committee of the Ethiopian Opposition Forces; published by MEDHIN, North American H.Q., Washington, D. C. 20005, U.S.A.), August 9, 1994.

Figure 12: (The late) The Rt. Hon. Prof. Asrat

ii) reports of the continuing abuses against the populace (as the recent arrest of **Prof. Asrat, Chairman of the All Amhara Peoples' Party (AAPP)**[10] and the war being waged in Ethiopia by **the Ethiopian Democratic Salvation Party/ MEDHIN's Ethiopian Salvation Army (ESA)**; [11]

iii) and the general outcry by the People of Ethiopia and the exiles here in the U.S.A. of the fraudulent nature of the elections.

In particular, We questioned him about the shootings in the Sheshamane area;[12] and further made him aware that We were aware of **the Ethiopian Chamber of Commerce (ECC)** backward and reactionary anti-dual citizenship stance, that formed a part of their submission to the Electoral Commission. [13] (The TGE's representative said he was unaware of all the above mentioned national and constitutional issues. We respectfully listened Mr. Fiffha's reiteration of the diplomatic

---

[10] See for example "STATE TERRORISM IS IN FULL SWING," **Ethiopian Register** (News Report), July 1994, pp. 15-16.

[11] See "The Ethiopian Salvation Army Conducts Military Operations Against TPLF/EPRDF," **Ethiopian Register**, April 1994, pp. 9-10; see also "Ethiopian Salvation Army continues its Military Assault," **Ethiopian Register**, June 1994, pp. 8-9.

[12] Op. cit, **Ethiopian Register,** June 1994, p. 9.

[13] See "Ethiopian Chamber of Commerce Proposes Constitutional Rights which Contradict the EPRDF's Draft Constitution," **Ethiopian Register,** June 1994, p. 11.

focused work objective thrust of the TGE's Permanent Mission to the U.N. - which makes the TGE's Office in Washington, the Mission that is answerable to these events and questionings).

There was a very intense discussion about the relevance/ inter-relatedness of **"pro-active dual citizenship"** with **Repatriation and Reparations**, and the very sensitive nature of Government-to-Government process that will have to be invoked and put into motion by Governments of the Continent and the diaspora for all three levels of implementation to be realized.

ETHIOPIAN SOVEREIGNTY by Birth/Blood:

"SELF DETERMINATION"

IN OUR ETHIO-DIASPORA COMMUNITY We still celebrate the day when His Majesty Haile Selassie I "laid the basis of the modern Government of Ethiopia,"[14] as he "freely gave of his own will" a Constitution to the Ethiopian Nation on **"Constitution Day, June 16th, 1931."**[15] It remains a day of celebration for Us for two specific reasons. One of which is, that, "It is worthy of note that this was the first instance in history where an absolute ruler had sought voluntarily to share sovereign authority with the subjects of his realm.."[16] Two, it is at this historical juncture that WE, THE PEOPLE, as "Ethiopians" - "Sovereigns and Nationals" were given THE RIGHT *"to share in the mighty task which [OUR] Sovereigns alone have had to accomplish in the past;"* thus, making it *"necessary for the modern Ethiopian to accustom himself to take part in the direction of all departments of the State..."*

---

[14] See CHAPTER VI LEGAL & CONSTITUTIONAL , subsection: PROMULGATING THE REVISED CONSTITUTION, in **SELECTED SPEECHES OF HIS IMPERIAL MAJESTY HAILE SELASSIE FIRST 1918 to 1967**, (The Imperial Ethiopian Ministry of Information Publication and Foreign Language Press Department, Addis Ababa, Ethiopia), 1967, p. 396.

[15] Op. cit, pp. 386-388.

[16] See **Ethiopian Liberation Silver Jubilee 1941-1966**, (Publication and Foreign Language Press Department, Ministry of Information, Addis Ababa - Ethiopia), 1966, pp. 121-122; see also ibid, ."..**THE QUEST OF ETHIOPIAN SOVEREIGNTY: AFRICAN NATIONHOOD AGENDA,"** p. 2.

With all of this in mind, and the further words and actions of Our Beloved Honorable Ancestor, Saint and Elder "Philosophic Statesman,"[17] **Marcus Mosiah Garvey**, who wisely instructed us to observe that: *"The State is all of us, and not a part of us.,"* [18]

---

[17] See Marcus Garvey (edited), **The Blackman**, Vol. 1, No. 6 Nov. 1934, p. 18; also in E.S.P. Mc Pherson B.A. (Hons.), **The Rt. Hon. "Marcus" Mosiah Garvey - The Black Moses & St. John The Divine; A Black Internationalist & "Philosophic Statesman's" Challenge to the State & Church, Educators & Our People. - A VOICE CRYING OUT IN THE WILDERNESS**, (Black International Iyahbinghi Press, Frankfield P. O., Clarendon, Jamaica), November 1980, pp. 15-16:
"Let the Government and Educators and Our People hearken to this 'PHILOSOPHIC STATESMAN,' and listen His [i. e. 'Marcus's'] Divine Reason: 'All of us cannot be ministers of the Gospel. Even the Apostles of Christ were divided up into different ranks and fulfilled different purposes. He had his Treasures, he had his Statesmen, and so we are satisfied to follow in the make up of his Cabinet, and therefore I am not taking the role of preacher, **but surely I am going to assume the role of philosophic statesmanship to lead my race through the wilderness of tears and to see to it that it is no longer charged or outdone by what heretofore was considered superior intelligence except by your own will of seeing the truth and doing the right**, because you have the same level of any man God ever made because he was just to endow you with the same faculties, the same senses, and more than all that, the same soul he gave to every other man in yours.'" [my emphases.]

[18] See "'10. Speech Delivered by Marcus Garvey on the steps of Ward Theatre, Kingston, Jamaica'" (from **The Blackman,** March 29, 1930), in Amy Jacques Garvey & E. U. Essien-Udom eds., **More Philosophy and Opinions of Marcus Garvey Vols., 3 Previously Unpublished Papers**, (Frank Cass and Company Ltd.), 1977, p. 737; also in ibid, Mc Pherson, **RASTAFARI and POLITICS..**, CHAPTER 9 The Politics of Liberation: Theocracy - a Developing Cultural Ideology, subsection called: Rastafari: A science of Government: A Theistic Ideology, p. 261.

Figure 13: TOP PHOTO: *H. I. M.* newly created Government, June, 1931, implied *He was the first Monarch* to democratize *His Throne*: Rastalogically, *Theocracy came to Earth.*

Figure 14: BOTTOM PHOTO The Rt. Hon. President General Marcus Garvey [second from right] reviewing a **UNIA & ACL** parade, in the 1922.

Figure 15: The Rt. Hon. *Saint* Marcus Mosiah Garvey, D.C.L/ Dr. of Civil Law; & D.D./Dr. of Divinity.

why We are so intensely involved in this constitutional quest, *"to set up a framework of law for the state."* So that, Our Peoples might follow this law meticulously, and that there be unity, peace, justice and development in Ethiopia and for ALL Ethiopians.

Having accepted the reality of the need for good Government and Governance of Ourselves through the due process of "the rule of law," Our "self-check" has led Us to the reclaiming of Our Birthright. [19] Our **Position Paper** as such is a symbolic and real act of protecting Our Sovereignty.

---

[19] See Rahim Botswana Bey (edited by Yusuf B. Tafari Bey), **I n I Self Law Am Master MOOR WISDOM**, (Rahim Bey) 1994, p. 5, Chapter Two Government, subsection: "**Self Check**: Ask you self this question: Where do I fit in, in order to sustain **Good Government** in this world that has become viscous reality? Remember: You are the reason for the season; you are the light of this world. Therefore Self-Government is your responsibility to your self and to your future,

The need for the Ethio-diaspora to reclaim Our Sovereignty also spells the obvious NEED for Us to reclaim THE LAND - the resources to the land. And thus, Our call upon you to become (further) actively involved in the realizations of Our **"REPATRIATION with REPARATION" quest**, is another cornerstone of Our **Position Paper**. It represents another of those silent-screams that You and Our other Continental Heads of States and diaspora kins - in authority - NEED NOW to address.

As Ethiopians and Pan-Africanist, Our concept of "Ethiopian Sovereignty" amounts to a "Pan-Ethiopianist" vision that **CHARGES** Your Honorable bodies and respectful selves to hear the voices of the Ethio-diaspora and to implement this wholesome perspective of **a Universal Ethiopianess**.

HELP US, YOUR NOW FOUND BROTHERS AND SISTERS crying in the wilderness!: *"So the poor hath hope, and iniquity stoppeth her mouth."* (Job 5 verse 16.)[20] So that We might establish, as **The Rt. Hon Marcus Mosiah Garvey** thundered: *"...a great and binding **racial hierarchy**, the founding of **racial empire** whose only natural, spiritual and political limits shall be God and 'Africa, at home and abroad.'"* [21]

We, My Honorable Brothers and Sisters, are collectively at this historical crossroads and **"Age of transition"**[22] that We

---

who equal the children. So, do your job and duty to preserve and uplift the Nation!"

[14] See **The Bible** (King James Version).

[21] See The Rt. Hon. Marcus Mosiah Garvey, **"African Fundamentalism A Racial Hierarchy and Empire for Negroes NEGRO'S FAITH must be CONFIDENCE IN SELF His Creed: ONE GOD ONE AIM ONE DESTINY,"** p. 1.

[22] ibid, H.I.M.'s "THRONE SPEECH [November 2] (1970," in **UTTERANCES..**, p. 245; also in Ras Everton/E.S.P. Mc Pherson, *"Rastafari, the Ethio-Diaspora and Ethiopia in this 'Age of Transition': The makings of A Pan-Ethiopianist Development March for Progress, Modernity and A Programme-of-Action Towards the 21st century.* A Paper presented at the First Rastafari/Ethiopian Cultural Celebration, on Saturday November 13, 1993, at International House,

find Ourselves serving Our Nation, are **CHARGED** with fulfilling the words of **The Hon. Prophet Marcus Mosiah Garvey**, when he said that Ethiopians (/Africans):

> "...the world over must practice one faith, that of Confidence in themselves, with One God! One Aim! One Destiny! Let no religious scruples, no political machination divide us, but let us hold together under all climes and in every country, making among ourselves a Racial Empire upon which 'the sun shall never set.' "[23]

We have now, an opportunity, to move beyond the "symbolic association" with "Power" that was mostly "ceremonial" for the Black Man and Woman. We MUST begin a Pan-Ethiopianization process through Constitutional Empowerment and Cultural Autonomy (i. e. independence, interdependence and intradependence) of Ethiopia, Africa and all Ethiopians scattered abroad. This highest level of the conscience-tization of the collective unconsciousness of Our Nation, that became blinded by the Euro/Eura-Africa illusion of 'the rule of law,' that led to the ideological imprisonment and cultural marginal-ization of Our people, led by an imposed elite trusteeship type of leaders throughout the World, will be best nullified by Our collective actions.

The state of affairs in Ethiopia since the overthrow of the Monarchial Government has led to a political cataclysm and fulfillment of that old adage, where: "every break up has its own rule." It has led to a state-of-affairs in which we have seen, and are now witnessing, desperate revolutionaries masking their absolute illusions in ideological and now 'eth-

---

Philadelphia.," **ETHIOPIA JAMAICA SOCIETY NEWS-LETTER**, Vol. 1 No. 2 Black History Month Special UNITY & DEVELOPMENT, Feb.-Mar. 1994, p. 22.

[23] Op. cit.

nic' cloaks, (seemingly) living on the fringe of a civic and constitutional crime.

To heal the breaches within Our Nation, Ethiopia and Our Continent: Africa, Ethiopia, MUST be successful in the process of remaking government, and in the democratic reconstruction and reorientation, while Our Honorable Statesmen and Women and gamut of skilled planners, bureaucrats and developers refine the natural interests of Our unique and diverse Peoples. Ethiopia, the unofficial diplomatic capital of Africa, and the **"permanent headquarters" of the OAU**,[24] **MUST** become **THE** Federal successful story of Our Continent, and ideal prelude to Our ultimate **"Confederation:" A SINGLE AFRICAN GOVERNMENT**.

---

[24] See H.I.M.'s STATEMENT TO THE 1963 AFRICAN SUMMIT, May 23, 1963, in ibid, **UTTERANCES OF H.I.M....**, p. 364.

AFRICAN NATIONHOOD: A UNION OF SOVEREIGN STATES

WE HAVE READ AND STUDIED with great interest one of the most structurally fundamental Paper of Our Continental and Worldwide struggle for Liberation put out by the OAU, entitled: **"AFRICA 2000 A Continental Government for Africa (6/1/92),"** that was supplied to a arm of one of Our constituency: the U. K. based **Ethiopian World Federation Incorporated Repatriation and Research Committee.** We would thus urge Your Honorable members of the Electoral Committee and the newly elected Constituent Assembly to arm themselves with this primary literate piece and to take note of its stated objectives, so that that this "Federal" harmonization can be successful in Ethiopia, and be adopted Continental-wide.

In particular, We further ask that you note keenly that with the June 1991 historic signing by the OAU Head of States and Governments, there was the establishing of the African Economic Commission (AEC), that was to come into formal existence **"2026."** The AEC's birth hinges upon "the harmonization of economic and financial policies," that in turn, **"would require the surrender, if only partially aspects of national sovereignty."**

The prelude and context to such awaited fruition was established - in the main - by Ethiopia, the founding and "the permanent seat" of the OAU. And the resolute call to this "continental wide programme,"

Figure 16: H.I.M. delivering the opening speech at the African Heads of State and Governments, Summit Conference, that led to the formation of the Organization of African Unity (O.A.U.), in Africa Hall, Addis Ababa, Ethiopia, May 23, 1963.

was made by none other than **His Majesty Haile Selassie I of Ethiopia**, at the birth of the OAU, May 26th 1963, in Addis Ababa, **Africa Hall**, when he thundered:

"...The organization of which We speak must possess a well-cumulated framework, having a permanent headquarters and an adequate Secretariat providing the necessary continuity between meetings of the permanent organs. It must include specialized bodies to work in particular fields of competence assigned to the organization. **Unless the political liberty for which Africans have so long struggled is complemented and bolstered by a corresponding economic and social growth, the breath of life which sustains our freedom may flicker out.** In our efforts to improve the standard of life of our peoples and to flesh out the bones of our independence, we count on the assistance and support of others. But this alone will not suffice, and, alone, would only perpetuate Africa's dependence on others.

A specialized body to facilitate and co-ordinate continent-wide economic programs and to provide the mechanism for the provision of economic assistance among **African nations** is thus required. Prompt measures can be taken to increase trade and commerce among us. **Africa's mineral wealth is great; we should co-operate in its development. An African Development Programme**, which will make provisions for the concentration by each **nation** on those productive activities for which its resources and its geographic and climatic conditions best fit it is needed. We assume that each African **nation** has its own national development programmes, and **it only remains for us to come together and share our experiences for the proper implementation of a continental-wide plan....**" [my emphases.][25]

This **Federal Continental Plan, MUST,** be demonstrated in Ethiopia, so that Ethiopians/Africans World-wide might move into the new millennia and fast coming twentieth century, in full confidence of re-claiming Our lost/forgotten "Sovereignty," and the making and achieving of Our own "Self Determination." This concept, practice and projected collective potency of "federalism" was graphically and cogently outlined by one of Our Son of the soil, the world renowned Scholar: Cheikh Anta Diop's, **"BLACK AFRICA The Economic and Cultural Basis for a Federated State"**

"..If we are to protect Black Africa..., **the idea of federation** must actually constitute - for all of us, especially those in high political position - **a method of**

---

[25] Ibid, **UTTERANCES..**, p. 356.

survival (by way of an efficacious political and economic organization to be set up in optimum time), not just a dilatory demagogic formulation receiving merely lip service.

We must stop fooling the masses with minor patchwork and bring about **the ultimate break with all the fake structures** *(Communaute,* Commonwealth, Eurafrica) which have no historical future. Black Africa must finally and definitively be started up the slope toward its **federal destiny.**

We cannot go on running with the hare and hunting with the hounds. **The African countries, in the years ahead, will be forced progressively to strengthen their organic federal ties** with ridding themselves of the remains of those that bind them still to their former 'mother countries.'.." (my emphases.) [26]

Put another way, the ultimate need and fruits of this federal system/Pan-Ethiopianization - as We see it - was best expressed in the words of the late Great African-American Scholar, **Dr. Chancellor Williams,**

"The federal system is the desired system for union among independent states for some overall common purpose, such as economic collaboration around which the spirit of brotherhood may be developed. **The Pan African movement is essentially a federal movement of this kind.**" (my emphases.)[27]

---

[26] See Cheikh Anta Diop (translated by Harold J. Salemson) , **BLACK AFRICA The Economic and Cultural Basis for a Federated State (with an interview by Carlos Moore)**, (Africa World Press edition) 1974; new expanded revision 1987, pp. 15-16.

[27] See Dr. Chancellor Williams (introduction by Baba El Senzengakulu Zulu Founder & Director of Ujamaa School), **THE REBIRTH OF AFRICAN**

Honorable Brothers and Sisters, Your Excellencies, We the ENF see Africa as the New Jerusalem, and Ethiopia as The Altar/the dwelling place and spring board of this Federal Developmental Plan.

This juncture of Our Paper thus brings Us to the role of A **"Constitutional Monarchy"/"The Crown"** in such a national Federal arrangement. We have read carefully the **"Paper on Basic Constitutional Concepts presented for Public Discussion,"** that was requested by the ENF from the TGE's representatives at the UN Permanent Mission, sent by the TGE's Ethiopian Election Committee, as they relate to this question, namely: **CHAPTER FOUR Unitary And Federal Government Structure And Power Division**, pp. 24-31, especially No. 50., p.24; No. 53, p.26; No. 72 **Constitutional Monarchy**, pp. 37-38, and No. 73 **Opinions of supporters of constitutional monarchy** pp. 38-39; No. 74. **Opinions of people not supporting a monarchial system limited by law**, pp. 74.

We also carefully read: **CHAPTER FIVE Various Government systems.**, especially No. 63 **Parliamentary government systems.**, pp. 32-33; No. 66 **Opinions of supporters of the parliamentary government system.**, pp. 33-34; No. 67 **Opinions of people opposing parliamentary government system.**, pp. 34-36. Because, The Crown is one of the executive element of an envisaged: "The Imperial Federal Democratic Government"/"Parliament." And as We said before: within the "Constitutional Draft" of August of 1974, while there was to be A Constitutional Monarchy, the locus of power was to remain in the Parliament. Our recognition of and advocating of the civil importance of a Parliamentary system, Parliamentarians and the electoral process was noted by His Majesty Haile Selassie I, as far back as December 10, 1968.

CIVILIZATION, (U. B. & U.S. COMMUNICATIONS SYSTEM, INC.), 1993, p. 127.

His profound and current relevant pointed wisdom should serve well Your Honorable members of the TGE's Electoral Commission and the newly elected Constituent Assembly - as they aim to move forward. His Majesty said:

> "Parliament as an institution was introduced in Ethiopia 38 years ago. The co-operation and collaboration of Our people in the implementation of the various laws passed by Our parliament over the years deserve merit and recognition...
>
> Parliament is an institution through which each and every Ethiopian serves for the common good and **unity of purpose**. As such the election should reflect this spirit. Parliamentarians must, above all, be imbued with a sense of patriotism and a sense of responsibility, for under the constitution, they are entrusted with legislation on social and economic development.
>
> ....Our parliament is one of the government organs entrusted with the well-being and **unity of the Ethiopian people**. In as much as improvements have been made in other branches of the government, so have the rules and procedures governing national elections been improved and implemented." (my emphases) [28]

---

[28] Ibid, GENERAL ELECTION, in **IMPORTANT UTTERANCES OF H.I.M. EMPEROR HAILE SELASSIE I**, (Published by The Imperial Ministry of Information, Addis Ababa, Ethiopia) 1972, pp. 172, 173, 174.

Figure 17: [r.-l.] *H. I. M.* and the late former Crown Prince of Ethiopia, H.I.H. Merd Azmatch Asfa Wossen Haile Selassie [; who was later elevated to: H.I.M. Amha Selassie I, Conquering Lion of the Tribe of Judah, Emperor of Ethiopia.]

Figure 18: TOP PHOTO: [l.-r.] H. I. M. and H.I.H. Merd Azmatch Asfa Wossen Haile Selassie.

Figure 19: BOTTOM PHOTO [r-l] [The late – and former] Crown Prince Asfa Wossen, and [then] Princess Medferiash Worq – his wife [who was later elevated and renamed – H. I. M. Medferiash Worq Abede].

Figure 20: TOP PHOTO [l-r] Princess Sifrash, Princess Mariam-Sena, H.I.M. Medferiash Worq Abede, H.I.H. Crown-Prince-Designate Zera Yacob, Princess Sihin, and H.I.M. Amha Selassie with his grand daughter, Ida.

Figure 21: BOTTOM PHOTO The late - H.I.H. Merd Azmatch Asfa Wossen Haile Selassie:/ H.I.M. Amha Selassie

Figure 22: TOP PHOTO His Imperial Highness Prince Ermias Sahle-Selassie Haile-Selassie, Grandson of HIM Emperor Haile Selassie I, and currently President of the Crown Council of Ethiopia, 1993.

Figure 23: BOTTOM PHOTO His Imperial Highness Prince Bekere Fikre-Selassie, Grandson of HIM Emperor Amha Selassie I, and currently Viceroy (Enderassé) of the Crown Council of Ethiopia, 1993

38   ETHIOPIAN SOVEREIGNTY: AFRICAN NATIONHOOD

Figure 24: TOP PHOTO H.I.H. Zere Yacob.

Figure 25: BOTTOM PHOTO H.I.H. Zere Yacob, Crown Prince of Ethiopia

Figure 26: TOP PHOTO: **THE CROWN & THE THRONE: [r.-l.]** H. R H. Prince Bekere Fikre-Selassie - Enderasse and Viceroy of The Crown Council of Ethiopia is greeted by Ras E.S.P. Mc Pherson - ENF Founder Chair/MOA Co-Chair (USA/Ja.)/ EJSNY Founder Co-Chair, at an Audience *given by The Crown Council of Ethiopia to the ENF/MOA (USA/Ja.)/EJSNY,* held in the Bronx, New York, USA, on the 29th of January, 1998; between 3.40 p. m.-6.45 p. m. At this historic meeting the ENF/EJSNY/ MOA (USA/Ja.) presented a working **"PRO-ACTIVE AGENDA,"** entitled, **"THE WATCHERS FROM WITHIN: THE THRONE & THE CROWN."** Here also, **the ENF Continental & Diaspora PRO-ACTIVE SOVEREIGN CONSTITUTIONAL AGENDA,** entitled: "...**World Leaders, what about Ethiopia?,** was ratified by *The Crown*

Figure 27: BOTTOM PHOTO: **ENF/MOA/EJSNY AUDIENCE WITH THE CROWN:** **[l-r]** Rases Claude, Mc Pherson, Dave; Sis. Amma; H.R.H. Prince Bekere Fikre-Selassie – *Enderasse* and *Viceroy of The Crown Council of Ethiopia*; Rases Bunny, Robert/Negus. (29/1/98.)

CONSTITUTIONAL MONARCHY / "CEREMONIAL FEDERALISM"

THE ENF AS WE SAID before, are "Royalists." We are all knowledgeable of **"the Laws of Succession,"**[29] as promulgated by the 1931/55/74 Constitution and thus **acknowledge the elevation of the former Crown Prince of Ethiopia, H.I.H. Merd Azmatch Asfa Wossen Haile Selassie, to: H.I.M. Amha Selassie I, Conquering Lion of the Tribe of Judah, Emperor of Ethiopia; and H.I.H. Prince Zera Yacob Amha Selassie, Crown Prince of Ethiopia**. We, along with The Royal Family of Ethiopia and The Crown Council of Ethiopia await the proper commemoration of this historic event, the coming day, as H.I.H. Amha Selassie wishes, when - in his own words:

> "... 'the actual Coronation Ceremony will be held, with the will of God Almighty, on Ethiopian soil **as and when the Ethiopian people regain their democratic freedoms with the sovereign dignity of Ethiopia remaining intact**, which can only be achieved as a result of the historic sacrifices of the gallant people of Ethiopia.'.." (my emphases.) [30]

---

[29] See ibid, Mc Pherson, **RASTAFARI and POLITICS..**, Constitutional Monarchy "Laws of Succession," pp. 161-164; p. 164: "INTERVIEW: Will Your Son succeed You on the Throne Your Imperial Majesty?
H.I.M.: **Why are you asking me this. If he can't inherit My Throne, why I say: 'Heir Apparent to The Throne for Ethiopia.'..**" [my emphases.]
See also Farika Birhan (Public Relations Chairperson), **"PRESS RELEASE Ethiopian International Unification Committee (Jamaica),"** March 1987:

[30] Ibid, **"The Message;"** in ibid, Mc Pherson, **RASTAFARI and POLITICS..**, p.180; See also Ras Everton Mc Pherson Co-Chairman of The Ethiopia Jamaica Society; Co-Chairman of Mo-Anbessa Provisional Steering Committee, "**Letter To: His Imperial Highness/Majesty Of Ethiopia Emperor Amha Selassie I, Her Imperial Highness Empress Medferiah Work Of Ethiopia, His Imperial**

We hold unswervingly to the Sovereign RIGHT's and historical truth that: 1) "...The Ethiopian Monarchy is an age-old, time honored institution which commands universal respect. Without its presence peace and tranquillity in Ethiopia cannot be ensured;..." 2) "...The Monarchy is above partisan politics which brings all political parties and organization under its all encompassing wings."

The role of the Constitutional Monarchy and the elected Parliament in this Federal Democratic Ethiopian state that was to follow in this post-Dergue period was clearly set out in **"The Message..,"** of H.I.H. Amha Selassie I:

> " A. The new Emperor proclaimed further that the Ethiopian people will eventually form **the new Imperial Federal Democratic Government** through the 'UNITED' struggle of **all** the Ethiopian People and the Democratic Forces of Ethiopia including the loyal members of the Ethiopian Armed Forces, fighting in all aspects to win the basic Freedom 'RIGHTS' of the Ethiopian people first, under whose **democratic reconstruction, a Federal Democratic Parliament, as the Supreme Legislative Body in the land, will be freely and democratically elected by the adult population of the Ethiopian people**. Legitimate power will then be exercised by the pluralist party or coalition parties that win the majority seats in the election to the Federal Parliament, and obtains the mandate to continue to govern legally, or to affect a change of government peacefully through the secret ballot...
>
> B. **The Emperor's role shall then revert to the onerous duties of a Constitutional Monarch as**

Highness Crown Prince Zera Yacob Amha Selassie I; c/o Bro. Dr. Getachew Mekasha, Private Secretary of His Imperial Majesty, [dated](September 4, 1992)."

custodian of the Ethiopian people's freedom and democracy and whose legitimate figure-head tasks, with its unifying historical and ceremonial functions shall be clearly stated limiting his political and administrative powers by the Federal Constitution that shall be approved by a 'Referendum' of the Ethiopian people.

This historical and quite successful **democratic marriages of respect to tradition, roots and indigenous culture with democratic freedoms and modernity** now exist in several advanced countries like Imperial Japan, United Kingdom, Sweden, Norway, to mention but few, that are the envy of many unfortunately oppressed nations of our time.

C. United and free, **Federal Democratic Ethiopia** shall then forge ahead her economic, social and political progress peacefully and harmoniously in a mixed but free economy, under the equal 'Rule of Law' that shall be drawn and promulgated by the 'Supreme' law making body of the Mother-Land, i. e. 'The People in the Federal Parliament', in peaceful co-existence and brotherly ties of all our good neighbors.

Each Federal State Legislature and State Administration, while united collectively at the Federal Government level for the common good and security of the Ethiopian people in the overall economic development, peaceful and conducive foreign affairs policy with strong defence of the freedom and sovereignty of Ethiopia as one and indivisible Nation enjoying equal and democratic individual freedoms of the inalienable human and political rights of the people of Ethiopia...." (my emphases.) (pp. 185-6.)[31]

It is this Imperial Federal Democratic Government that We have dubbed as: **"Ceremonial Federalism."** [32] (A process, when extended to the Ethio-Diaspora, will constitutionally empower Our scattered Nation with a new nation status.)

As later Mo-Anbessa literate sources pointed out: "...**The weight and moral authority of the Monarchy can usefully coexist and compliment a democratically elected government;..**"[33] and The Crown/"Moa-Anbessa pledges its full support to all democratic forces both within and outside

---

[31] See **"RIGHT THE SECRETARIAT OF The United Ethiopian National Solidarity Supreme Council For the Freedom RIGHTS of the Ethiopian People to The Imperial Ethiopian Federal Democratic Government. PRESS RELEASE,"** April 1989/ "The Message..." ; "The Message..," is also in, **OUR OWN** *The Pan Africanist Movement of Jamaica International Magazine*, Vol. 1 No. 1 March-June 1990, pp. 3-6; also in ibid, Mc Pherson, **RASTAFARI and POLITICS..**, pp. 180-188.

[32] Ibid, Mc Pherson, **RASTAFARI and POLITICS..**, CHAPTER 10 Towards the Beginnings of A New Ethiopia: The Restoration of the Solomonic Dynasty and "The Constitutional Monarchy," p. 302.

[33] See **"'MO-ANBESSA' THE CONQUERING LION Press Release,"** June 1991: ."..Mo-Anbessa is an ad-hoc created body created by patriotic Ethiopians dedicated to the establishment of a constitutional monarchy in Ethiopia. Mo-Anbessa strongly believes that the only way that will guide Ethiopia through a transitional period to a full fledged democracy without further bloodshed and fratricidal strife is the immediate return to Ethiopia of H.I.M. Amha Selassie I. The Ethiopian Monarchy is an age-old, time honored institution which commands universal respect. Without its presence peace and tranquillity in Ethiopia cannot be ensured.

The Emperor is the Symbol of the State and of the Unity of the people deriving his position from the will of the people with whom resides sovereign power. **The weight and moral authority of the Monarchy can usefully coexist and compliment a democratically elected government** as for example, in Great Britain or Japan.

The Monarchy is above partisan politics which brings all political parties and organization under its all encompassing wings. As such, Mo-Anbessa welcomes everybody's participation in all its activities...;" See also, ibid, Mc Pherson, **RASTAFARI and POLITICS...,** pp. 301-302.

Ethiopia who are dedicated to the cause of building a pluralistic society and a market-driven economy." [34]

As We said in Our opening statement, We wholeheartedly support this attempt to return Ethiopia to a truly democratic path, and again We wish to echo the wise words of warning of H.I.H. Amha Selassie, and point them to the TGE - Electoral Commission, the newly elected Constituent Assembly and the banned political parties (and other formations that have opted not to participate in this process):

> "....But in order to achieve her potential for greatness, peace, democracy and liberty are the pre-conditions. War must cease. The people of Ethiopia must be given a chance to develop peacefully and must have a say in the type of their government. Political and ideological differences must be solved through **the ballot and not the bullet. Any organization or group must seek the support of the people to achieve their political aims and not strive to impose their will on the people.**
>
> ......On our part, in so far as Monarchy is the symbol of their unity and stability, and if the people so desire, we are willing and ready to serve them as a symbol of constitutional monarchy. We are committed to work with **any party elected by the people**, and do everything in our power to ease their **transition to true democracy** which is not going to be an easy matter in the present circumstances.

---

[34] See also "**'MO-ANBESSA' THE CONQUERING LION A CALL TO RALLY ALL ETHIOPIANS,**" 1991, p. 2: ."..Mo-Anbessa is not a political party or organization with its own separate political or partisan agenda. Mo-Anbessa is an ad hoc body created for the specific purpose of restoring the Ethiopian Monarchy to its rightful place in Ethiopian political order of things....

Mo-Anbessa pledges its full support to all democratic forces both within and outside Ethiopia who are dedicated to the cause of building a pluralistic society and a market- driven economy."

May the Almighty God help Ethiopia." [my emphases.] [35]

These words and perspective which We fully share, were reiterated by Our Honorable Chairman of Mo-Anbessa, Dr. Getachew Mekasha, in a article entitled, **"LET ETHIOPIA BE ETHIOPIA":**

> "....Ethiopia's deliverance and salvation demands for all to put now the country's interest above all other considerations, to cast aside petty jealousies and narrow parochialism and join hands to save the nation from fragmentation and outmoded Marxist oppression.
>
> Moa Anbessa believes the only way that will guide Ethiopia through these difficult times to a full-fledged democracy without further bloodshed and fratricidal strife is the immediate establishment of a Constitutional Monarchy in Addis Abeba. This age-old, time honored and universally respected home-grown Ethiopian institution had withstood the test of time. Ethiopian unity and historical continuity is best symbolized by the monarchy. Fulfilling its traditional role of national standard bearer, a fully restored Ethiopian Monarchy will, as it has always done in the past, provide the all-encompassing umbrella under which all national activity will once again flourish. The weight and moral authority of the monarchy not only can usefully coexist and compliment a democratically elected government, but will also act as an anchor and stabilizing force at all times..." [36]

---

[35] See also **"STATEMENT BY HIS IMPERIAL MAJESTY AMHA SELASSIE I REGARDING THE OPPORTUNE SITUATION IN ETHIOPIA,"** 1991, p. 2.

[36] **The Ethiopian Examiner,** May 1993, p. 15.

We are well aware of the many declared and masked discomforts of many of the social (/ethnic) and political constituencies in Ethiopia towards the "ceremonial efforts" of The Crown, in its legitimate assertion to remain the major element in a balance of alliances/celebration of diversities and unity. We are also well aware of the deep and ingrained hatred of Monarchist by Communists - revisionists! **Notwithstanding, The Crown, Mo-Anbessa, the Rastafari international community, and the concerned Ethio-Americas Peoples - as the ENF represents, are "The Civil Guardians" of Ethiopian Sovereignty!** For Us, the diaspora has to be released and incorporated into the process of Ethiopia's constitutional renewal - and thus this challenge from the diaspora, for active inclusion in the civil life of Ethiopia and Our Continent.

MULTI-PARTY DEMOCRACY: ETHIO-DIASPORA ELECTORAL INVOLVEMENT

AT THE (already mentioned) presentation made by the EJS/Moa-Anbessa Co-Chairman, Ras Everton Mc Pherson, at the demonstration held at Columbia University, that was called by *the Ethiopian Patriotic Organizations*, on Saturday, March 19th, 1994, Our demands for active participation by **"A COMMON FRONT:"** the ENF/Ethio-Diaspora in the electoral system of Ethiopia was explicitly made as one of the needed prescriptives to fully liberate Ethiopia was outlined:

"4) This Front [i.e. the ENF] MUST DEMAND that, in the future, when a national legitimate transitional regime is put in power by The People, that the make up of a **"real"** Constituency Assembly includes exiled Ethiopians - who should be able to vote in such a process, as too, therefore participate in any electoral procedures relating to the collective Sovereignty and welfare of the Ethiopian People/Our Continent: Africa."[37]

This position for pro-active Ethio-diaspora electoral involvement was earlier put forth to the recently exiled and concerned New York based Ethiopian community, and banned-exiled Ethiopian political parties, as **MEDHIN**, by EJS/Moa-Anbessa Co-Chair, Ras Mc Pherson, at the regular held **"ETHIOPIAN TOWN MEETING,"** at Columbia University, on July 25th, 1993; and August 7th, 1993, respectively.[38]

Locally, the call for a **"Parliamentary Theocracy"** put forth by **the Royal Judah Coptic Ethiopian Church**, in their **"EATUP Manifesto,"**[39] and the submission by **the Jamaica**

---

[37] Ibid, Mc Pherson, **"ETHIOPIA: ONE NATION - MANY PEOPLES...,"** p. 6.

[38] See **"TOWN MEETING on THE CURRENT SITUATION IN ETHIOPIA With Emphasis on the Ethiopian Academic Community and Human Rights Violations Guest Speakers: Among the Illegally Dismissed Addis Ababa University Faculty Members. Professor Solomon Terfa Former Head, Political Science Department. Professor Meskerem Abebe, 1-5 p.m., Sunday, JULY 25, 1993, Horace Mann Hall at Teachers College, Columbia University, New York, NY."** See also **"AN ETHIOPIAN TOWN MEETING at Columbia University Co-sponsored By THE AFRICAN STUDENTS ASSOCIATION AND MEDHIN. 'The Current Situation in Ethiopia with Emphasis on Peace, Democracy, and Human Rights Violations By Col. Goshu Wolde Chairman of Medhin..,' Saturday, August 7, 1993, Columbia University, Teachers College, Horace Mann Hall."** Present also and contributing also at this historic gathering, was **Ras Ridi**, President of **the Iniversal Rastafari Inity (IRI)**, a new York based Rastafari Internationalist Ethiopianist formation, and one of the main affiliates of the EJS/Moa-Anbessa.

[39] See The Royal Ethiopian Judah Coptic Church political manifesto, entitled, **"The Ethiopian-African Theocracy Union Policy (EATUP) True Genuine Authentic Policy: (FIOCAP),"** 1984, that was presented to the then (one party -

Progressive League, calling for a **"Monarchial Republic,"** made in the constitution review exercise,[40] among many other advocating of a Royalist stance,[41] all point to the relevance and need for, the Restoration of The Crown in Ethiopia. In the words of Our other Honorable EJS/Moa-Anbessa Co-Chair, **Ras Howard Goulbourne**:

> "....Rasta/Jamaicans provides an institutional base to assist in the restoration of the Solomonic Dynasty on one half of the Ethiopian global political diameter, while The Crown itself provides a symbol of unity to Jamaica's new sovereign status, on the other. Hence the need to restore is seen as the common political line going East to West, the radius connecting Jamaicans and scattered Ethio/Africans to the rising of the black empire..."[42]

Jamaica Labour Party) government, call for a "A twin legislative, Parliamentary Constitutional Monarchy; maintaining the constitutional concept of constructive Parliamentary Opposition, loyal to Nation Interests; through the National Ombudsman Parliamentary Opposition, Parliamentary Regional Executive, Parish Councils, Regional Executive Constituent Councils, National Legislature, and a National Ministerial Cabinet, consisting of eighteen (18) portfolios." (ibid, Mc Pherson, **RASTAFARI..**, p. 289). See also ibid, Mc Pherson, **RASTAFARI and POLITICS..**, Chapter 9, section called **EATUP: The Royal Ethiopian Judah Coptic Church 1984-1988**, pp. 288-290. See also Alston Barry Chevannes, **Social and Ideological Origins of the Rastafari Movement in Jamaica**, (Submitted in partial fulfillment of the requirement for the degree Doctor of Philosophy under the executive Committee of the Graduate Schools of Arts and Science, Columbia University, 1989), pp. 414-416.

[40] See **"The Jamaica Progressive League Kingston, Jamaica Renewed,"** (1989), call for the ."..adoption of a Republican Constitution"/"Monarchial Republic;" plus See "Preamble to a summary proposal for constitutional change," **The Jamaica Record**, June 12, 1991, p. 7; see also ibid, Mc Pherson, **"Letter to H.I.M., H.I.M. & Crown Council of Ethiopia...,"** (September 4, 1992), **4. National Liberation and the Ethio-Jamaican Community.**, pp. 3-4

[41] See for example Bro. A. Foxe, Rasta participation in Jamaican politics," **The Daily Gleaner**, (Letter to the Editor), July 21, 1988, p. 6; ibid, Mc Pherson, **RASTAFARI and POLITICS....**, p. 285, p. 295.

[42] See Howard Gouldbourne (Book Review), "Rastafari and Politics Pt. 1 & Pt. 11," **The Jamaica Record**, January 1992, p. 7; January 3, 1992, p. 7; see also Ikael Tafari, **RASTAFARI and the GRENADA REVOLUTION: From Cultural Resistance to Political Liberation Completing the Second Cycle**, (Unpublished

The logical formation of the ENF, thus, adds to the base and breath of this "institutional base/political diameter/ new sovereign status." It now encompasses the Ethio-Americas and other Ethiopians (Africans) scattered globally.

The real genesis that has led to this position of the ENF, rest within Our recognition for "the rule of (constitutional) law" and its "application;" and Our uttermost concern for the welfare of Our People/scattered Nation. This is why for example, within the local and international Rastafari Community there as been a lot of "constitutional approaches" in Defence of Our People.[43] In the words of one of these earliest Ethio-cultural internationalist, **Bro. Asento Foxe**, in 1960, it is these constitutional concerns on behalf of Our Peoples, that amount to a political quest/practice, that are wholesomely qualified as an affirmative prerogative of Our Community to enact:

Paper, Cave Hill, University of the West Indies, Barbados), 1992, pp. 7-8; footnote 5 p. 36.

[43] See [Ras] Mortimer Planno, "West Indies Federation a Make-Shift," **African Opinion** (Letter to the Editor) July-August 1958; see Mortimer Planno, (Jamaica W. I.), "Repatriation - A Human's Right," **African Opinion**, Vol. 4 Mar.-April 1959 Nos. 11 & 12, pp. 6-7; see Martimo Planno, "Back to Ethiopia," **The Daily Gleaner** (Letter to the Editor), January 15, 1962, pp. 6-7.

Ras Sam Brown's, is the first Rastaman that ran in the 1961 elections. His Black Man's Party manifesto of 1961, that was patterned off **the Millard Johnson's Garveyite Peoples Progressive Party (PPP)** manifesto, all called for a Republican type constitution: see "'Assembly Sunday' - to form Party," **The Star**, February 7, 1961; also in ibid, Mc Pherson, **RASTAFARI and POLITICS...**, section called Beginnings of A Modern Ethiopianist Emancipatory Movement: Bro. Sam Brown to Bro. 'Wally' Rodney, p. 271.

Ras Dr. Steve Mc Donald's Jamaica Liberation Movement political manifesto of 1980, that formed the basis of him contesting the General Election of 1980, which made him the second Rastaman to contest an election in Jamaica, called for a Republican constitution, where: ."..Black People involving Rastafari, be fully recognized as the grassroots emphasis as a strategy for developing the country on a permanent basis. That Black People be accepted as the majority Culture; to promote a proper motto: 'OUT OF ONE GOD, MANY PEOPLES and RACES and CULTURES.'" See also Steve Mc Donald, **"The Question of Race and the Concept of Liberation,"** (1987), p. 23; also in ibid, Mc Pherson, **RASTAFARI and POLITICS..**, section called The Jamaica Liberation Movement (JLM): 1972-8.

> "It would be foolish to ignore the risk of letting such conditions prevail to nourish the seeds of a revolution which is bound to overtake a community which is so indifferent to the suffering and misfortunes of a large number of their people. Surely this cannot be the will of God for man?"[44]

So overwhelming is this imperative to be active democratic participants in the civil life of Our People through political practice, that at the First Rastafari International Theocracy Assembly held in Canada, 1982, there was a collective communal resolve that read

> "It has been debated for a long time and will continue to be debated, 'Should a Rastafarian be politically involved?' In this time it has been agreed that political involvement is imminent in order for I and I to protect our interests. Our interests lies in the welfare of our people."[45]

---

[44] See A. Foxe, **"The Rastafarians Past and Present,"** (A. Foxe, The Secretary, Jamaica Working Committee, Sub-Local 37, Ethiopian World Federation Inc., London W10,79 Chesterton Road), p.10, in ibid, Mc Pherson, **RASTAFARI...**, p.261. Please note Bro. Asento Foxe is the present **International President of the Imperial Ethiopian World Federation, Inc. (IEWF)** and the Head Spiritual Adviser of **The Church of Haile Selassie I**. His earliest activities in the U.K., that broadened the international spectrum of this Ethio-diaspora link can be read/seen in: the late 1960's activities of **Bros. Foxe and Gabriel 'Blue' Adams**, neo-Garveyite **Universal Black Improvement Organisation (UBIO)**, in U.K., with a political wing called: **the People's Democratic Party (PDP)**; by 1971 UBIO transformed into EWF local., and a second EWF local in 1972; see ibid, Mc Pherson, **RASTAFARI and POLITICS...**, p. 272; see Ernest Cashmore, **Rastaman The Rastafarian Movement in England**, (George Allen & Unwin), 1979, p.51; see Jah Bones, **One Love Rastafari: History, Doctrines & Livity**, (Voice of Rastafari Publishers), 1982, p. 40; see "Rastafarians in Jamaica and Britain," **NOTES & REPORTS Catholic Commission for Racial Justice**, No. 10 January 1982, p. 7.

[45] **"Report on the First International Rastafarian Conference held in Toronto, Ontario, Canada July 23rd-July 25th, 1982 'Unification of Rastafari,' Workshop NO. 4 RASTAFARI and education within the political and economic system,' Politics,"** p. 20; op. cit, **RASTAFARI and POLITICS...**, p. 261.

It is the suffering and misfortunes of Ethiopia (and Africa) that are Our concerns. It is the interests and welfare of Ethiopia that We are here seeking to determine and protect by way of Our Ethio-diaspora input into this constitutional draft process. We aim to help the shaping of a reformed multi-party democracy, that will amount to a newly won sovereign nation status for the Ethio-diaspora.

It is here that the old adage: **"ignorance is no excuse,"** moves Us to enlighten Your Honorable Excellencies, about the earliest Ethiopianist Emancipatory cognition's and phases of this constitutional approach by Our Ethio-Jamaican community. For, what the (so-called) 'independent' movement/'flag independence' in Jamaica (and throughout the Caribbean islands and Americas) avoided, was the issue of "RACE"/IDENTITY! So while Jamaica hurriedly moved towards the building of a miniature model of a "....Britain, American or a European - type state,"[46] rather than building on the "cultural traditions" of Our African past, the Rastafari Movement questioned the government-of-the-day and society at large about the Peoples national standing and the application of justice and equality for ALL. **Ras Martimo Planno's**, "Back to Ethiopia," a letter to the Editor, of January 1962, asked

---

[46] See Katrin Norris, **The Search for an Identity**, (Institute of Race Relations; London; Oxford University Press), 1962, p. 72, p. 88; also See E.S.P. Mc Pherson, **The Positive Relationship Between Religion and Cultural Development: A Case Study of Rastafari**, (A Sociology of Development M.Sc. Draft, Sociology Department, Mona, University of the West Indies, Kingston, Jamaica), 1988/9; 90-91; subsection called **Review of Ethnographic and Developmental Literature on Rastafari**, pp. 14-31.

Figure 28: Ras Martimo Planno - one of the earliest Rastafari Intellectual and Pan-Africanist of the mid 1950s to late 1960s.

"....What provisions will be made within the New constitution for the desire of those who alienate themselves from the Jamaica way of life? I am thinking principally of those who desire is to be repatriated to Ethiopia. One of the countries of Africa that already granted lands for the sole purpose of resettling people from the Western world. I as one who is claiming by originality (Ethiopian) would like the world to know that our rights must be respected. Because I am of the opinion that respect for man's right is the greatest achievement of peaceful solution to problems which has a temperature of 100 degrees.

Major problem - will the Government tell us what are the plans for the Rastafarians who are Ethiopians? Independence mean nothing to people who claim a different nationality to the country in which he or she resides. Will Jamaica's Government study the articles of right which must not be suppressed by statutory laws..." [47] (my emphases.)

---

[47] Ibid, **The Daily Gleane**, Jan. 15, 1962, p. 8.

These said questions surrounding Our cultural identity/ nation status/Sovereignty are now posed to Your Honorable Electoral Commission, newly elected Constituent Assembly, and the Ethiopian Nation at large!

The realization of Our quest to legally democratically participate in Our Nation's civil life and development, will be best activated and institutionalized through the granting of "dual citizenship" rights to the Ethio-diaspora. Thus, We were indeed hearkened to see that this question of "dual citizenship" was/is been discussed by the general populace in this constitutional exercise now on-going.

"ACTIVE" DUAL CITIZENSHIP RIGHTS:
Elected by "Birth/Blood"

As WE SAID BEFORE, the questions surrounding what criteria's would amount to "dual citizenship" rights, were discussed at the Electoral Commission exercise hosted by the TGE's UN staff at Columbia University. Numbers 67-69, ranging from: by birth; blood; and or, both, were offered. Number 69 was chosen..

What We found more interesting however, on "nationality"/"dual citizenship" was contained in your, **"...Paper on Basic Constitutional Concepts presented for Public Discussion..,"** CHAPTER SIX Other items to be included in a Constitution., Nos. 76 & 77, **Nationality**, pp. 40-41. on p. 40, No. 76, in part says firstly:

> "....The citizenship principle that exists in the Ethiopian law is blood relationship. However, if it is confirmed that a citizen of another country **has lived in Ethiopia and can speak the country's official language and has adequate ability**, he can be granted Ethiopian citizenship..." (my emphases.)

Secondly, No. 76, continued:

> ".....The existing citizenship law has one anti democratic feature. It does not regard man and women as equals. If an Ethiopian man marries a foreign woman, he will not forfeit his Ethiopian citizenship and the Ethiopian citizenship rights of children born of the two are also guaranteed. His foreign wife also becomes an Ethiopian citizen for merely being married to an foreigner and the law of her husbands country can make her a citizen of that country, **she loses her**

Ethiopian citizenship without the provision of any alternative choice. Her children will also remain to be citizen of their father's country...." (my emphases.)

Thirdly, and more important to the objective thrust of Our Position Paper, No. 77, on p. 41, stated:

"...The dual citizenship question is not to be decided only by a constitution or law of one country. If the law of one country allows dual citizenship and the constitution or law of the other does not, the citizen of one country cannot obtain the right of dual citizenship. **This means this right can be applicable when there is similar law between the two countries...**" (my emphases.)

The ENF's position on these three point are:

Firstly, for Us in the Diaspora, many of whom have never "lived in Ethiopia," and are not - as of yet - learnt in "the country's language" (Amharic) - "adequately," such is not a valid basis not be incorporated as Nationals/citizens of Ethiopia. Moreover, as the question of an "official" language is one of the issues been discussed with respect to the creation of a multi-ethnic and multi-religious federal state, the speaking of the "Amharic" language, should NOT be a criteria for citizenship. Already, Ethiopia has to be now reconciling itself with the absurd notion built around the 'ethnic' groupings of political blocs/"regions" , that are based on the commonality of language(s), religions, ideological stances and other cultural differences. And thus, the cultural struggles surrounding ethno-linguistics should NOT be a criteria for citizenship. To the ENF, the notion of "ethnicity" (that includes qualifications by linguistics) can be used as a working paradigm for the understanding of human diversities. [48] Here again, We point to the working relevance of the ENF's motto: "**....UNITY IN DIVERSITY..**"

Secondly, the ENF decries vehemently the sexist nature of the former non-recognition of Ethiopian women, who marry peoples of other nationalities. The Ethio-diaspora family structure was destroyed - if not - structurally altered, by way of slavery and colonialism. Our families here in the Diaspora are matri-focally led. This brings in that ancient characteristic matriarchal value factor, that is non-existent in the euro-nuclear family model enunciated by the system, and unsuccessfully attempted by Our people. Here in the diaspora the primary mode of characterization and operation is captured in that primary Afro-Caribbean literate source on the family, written by **Edith Clarke**, entitled: **My Mother Who Fathered Me.** To the ENF, The Ethiopian Woman **MUST** be legally empowered to maintain that nation status of her "Ethiopianess" - the same as her children.

Thirdly, as We said before: only **the comprehensive application of "dual citizenship"** by respective Heads of States/Governments-of-the-day on the Continent and throughout the diaspora can bring about the real fruition of Ethiopia's

---

[48] See Yosef Ford, "**ETHIOPIA: IN SEARCH OF A NATIONAL IDENTITY Africans Cannot Liberate Themselves from,**" Themselves, (1993), pp. 6-7; p. 11: ."..the important thing is that all the peoples of Ethiopia share a number of archaic culture features derived from a pan-African and pan-Cushitic cultural substratum beneath the present politically exploited and more or less artificial bounding indices of socio-cultural clusters defined as 'ethnic,' 'tribal,' or 'national' groups. This does not mean, by any measuring standard, and by ideological oversimplification in particular, that there is such a thing as 'Ethiopian culture.' **That what is meant here is that there is a common denominator which is overlaid by a multitude of converging cultural variants-- religious, linguistic, and social further linked by territorial contiguity.** That which is disconnecting today, is the attempt to disregard the development of this complex configuration by viewing the relationships between different groups through an inadvertent western prism and the attempt to redefine these inter-cultural relationships in a similar if not exact fashion as it was during the colonial domination of Africans and other Third World peoples.." (my emphases).

(/Africa's) scattered Peoples reclaiming their due rights of Sovereignty/Nationality (Originality). With Your Honorable members establishing this law, such will set the tone for the rest of the Continent and the Diaspora to follow.

Without being repetitive, We will now share Our in put on this quest for "dual citizenship," that was outlined at the constitutional exercise, held at Columbia:

THE QUESTION OF "DUAL CITIZENSHIP"

MC PHERSON: ...Firstly, if I am to interpret "67:" "by blood," as meaning: **"Race,"** and as a anthropological reference - as the word: **"Ethiopia"** is - because in the very **Dictionary**, it says: **"one of the races of man."** Moreover, let Us refer to the history:, ahm, in 1961 when the first **"Mission"** from the West visited Ethiopia, it was His Majesty Haile Selassie I that said: he realized that slaves had were sent from Ethiopia, to Jamaica. [49]

Secondly, when he came to Jamaica in 1966 [April], he referred to Jamaicans and Ethiopians as been: **"Blood Brothers."** [50] So, in that sense, if the

---

[49] See **REPORT OF MISSION TO AFRICA,** (The Government Printer, Duke Street, Kingston), 1961, pp. 16-17: .":..Speaking Amharic which was interpreted by the Minister of the Imperial Guard, H.I.M. told us that he knew the black people of the West and particularly Jamaica, were blood brothers to the Ethiopians and he knew that slaves were sent from Ethiopia to Jamaica...;" See also, E.S.P. Mc Pherson B.A. (Hons.), "TIME OF JUBILEE AND RESTORATION," **GAFFAT ETHIOPIA** Amharic and English Monthly Newspaper, July 1993, Vol. 2 No. 3, pp. 1, 8, 11; also in **The Herald (Jamaica)**.

[50] See "Emperor addresses both House of Parliament: Selassie stresses importance of co-operation between smaller states," **The Daily Gleaner**, April 22/23, 1966; which is also in: "HAILE SELASSIE ADDRESSES THE PEOPLE," **JAHMUG Centenary Edition**, (JAHMUG, P. O. Box 772, London SW11 5XY, 1991), pp. 6-7, 22; see also **ETHIOPIA JAMAICA SOCIETY NEWSLETTER**, Vol. 1 No. 1 Black History Month Special Feb.-March 1992, p. 1; see also **"The reply of HIS IMPERIAL MAJESTY EMPEROR HAILE SELASSIE 1st. OF ETHIOPIA to Donald Sangster P.M. of Jamaica At the National Stadium, Kingston Jamaica. At the National Stadium, Kingston, Jamaica 21st April, 1966,"** (in, **E.I.U.C. Newsletter**, 133 Tower Street, Kingston, Jamaica, p. 1).

word **"blood,"** is there, it must be seen as an anthropological and a "Racial" reference.

In that instance, I would choose "69" - in the respect that, ahm - whether you are born in Ethiopia - as part of the Rastafari Community is in Shashamane, Ethiopia, and

In that instance, I would choose "69" -   in the respect that, ahm - whether you are born in Ethiopia - as part of the Rastafari Community is in Shashamane, Ethiopia, and We expect to be in Our Homeland, then in a dual sense it could be held together through "69."

Just to stress a little on the "blood relationships:" also in the 15th century, We have historical proof that: People left - by free-will from Ethiopia to Jamaica, while the Zagwe Dynasty had disrupted the Solomonic Dynasty. And they returned back Triumphantly to Ethiopia!.

So there is that connection there also betwixt Us.

So I would say that: in respect of   **"dual citizenship,"** We should see such in a **"Pan-Africanist"** sense. Not just for A People who want to go-back-to-Ethiopia. But as, the question was already raised by His Majesty in 1963 at the OAU, where ALL PEOPLE who are **"Africans,"** have the right to "dual citizenship"; and, in that: His Majesty Haile Selassie I had also said in the Jamaica Parliament, in 1966, that: special provisions were made for Jamaicans in the **OAU Charter**. [51]

---

[51] Ibid, **"The reply of His Imperial Majesty Emperor Haile Selassie 1st of Ethiopia to Donald Sangster, P. M. of Jamaica, at the National Stadium, Kingston, Jamaica, 21st April, 1966;"** also see ibid, Mc Pherson, **RASTAFARI and POLITICS..**, pp. 312-3, footnote 52.; also see **ETHIOPIA JAMAICA SOCIETY NEWSLETTER**, Vol. 1 No. 1 Feb.-Mar. 1992, pp. 1-2.]

So I would go along with "69" here.

Figure 29: UPON H. I. M. VISIT TO JA.: "Arrival – Adoring Crowds Breaks Protocol [April 21, 1966]."

Figure 30: STATE VISIT OF H. I. M. HAILE SELASSIE TO JAMAICA: Pictured at King's House are His Imperial Majesty Haile Selassie I - Emperor of The Kingdom of Ethiopia (3rd from Right); His Excellency Sir Clifford, G.C.M.G., G.C.V.D. - Governor General of Jamaica representing The Queen of Jamaica (2nd from Right). Others are (L-R-R) Her Royal Highness Imebet Sofiya Desta - Granddaughter of H. I. M.; Her Excellency Lady Campbell (Wife of The Governor-General); Mrs. E. Kean - Lady-in-Waiting to Her Excellency Lady Campbell and daughter of Sir Clifford and Lady Campbell; and His Highness Prince Mikael - Grandson of His Imperial Majesty.

Figure 31: HAPPY CRUSH: The pressures of the masses were terrific everywhere. 'COURIER' Cameraman got this crush-squeezing shot of His Imperial Majesty followed by Governor-General Sir Clifford Campbell and a very protective Brigadier General Assefa Demise, Principal Aide-de-Camp to His Imperial Majesty

Figure 32: **AT OFFICIAL CEREMONY:** In the Royal Box His Imperial Majesty heard Welcoming Addresses and fittingly replied. H. I. M. pictured in the course of His reply.

THE ERITREAN SECESSIONIST ACT and DUAL CITIZENSHIP

MC PHERSON: Through the Chair: We don't want the question of "dual citizenship," be, mixed with **"the Eritrea issue."**
YOU CANNOT BE IN ETHIOPIA AND WANT "DUAL CITIZENSHIP"!, Right! THAT ACT OF ERITREA IS **A "DISINTEGRATING ACT."**
So, I know that many people are trying to use it as a rationale - you know - to say that: "dual citizenship" could mean, you could say: you are Eritrean with your own 'autonomy,' or, so called: 'self determination' - and still be a part of Ethiopia! THAT CANNOT WORK! YOU ARE ALREADY IN ETHIOPIA! [**The People APPLAUSE/P. A.**]

THE REINSTITUTION OF THE LAND: REPATRIATION WITH REPARATION KEY

IN THIS BID FOR CONSTITUTIONAL renewal and order, the most fundamental human right is the Peoples due right to **THE LAND**. There **MUST** be a reinstitution/restitution of the lands that were illegally seized between 1974-1991 (-1994). For Us in the diaspora, this is one of Our main concern, as a number of the ENF constituencies - on the ground in Ethiopia (as the EWF, Inc. and the Nyahbinghi Order of His Majesty) - and affiliations (as the Queen of Sheba & Pharaohs

Masonic Movement), have a direct need for the restitution of lands earlier rightfully given to Us for developmental projects.

Also, Your Honorable Excellencies must realize that it is with the reinstitution of the land, that the hope for Repatriation with Reparation will be made real and possible to be fulfilled. Again, in this regard - Ethiopia **MUST** become the typesetter for this ingathering and empowering of Our Peoples in the diaspora and the continent. The REPATRIATION of Our People who are so desirous to come home MUST be a carefully ordered and worked out process. Our continental and diasporic age-old demands for REPARATION, that is a current prioritized agenda of the OAU and a number of constituencies within the Americas, will complement this envisaged Exodus.

The importance of THE LAND - THE REINSTITUTION OF THE LAND and its logical colliery, REPATRIATION, was recently expressed by Us in a forthcoming, "**POSITION PAPER ON REPATRIATION, TO THE O.A.U., FROM THE [ENF/] ETHIOPIA JAMAICA SOCIETY (EJS INC.*)** [52] **[EJSNY]**. Our words remain a challenged to Your Honorable Excellencies to constitutionally implemented and to be tackled immediately by any respective government-of-the-day, democratically elected by ALL the people of Ethiopia:

"....Acknowledging that THE BASE MUST BE UPON THE LAND (for historically as Ethiopians [Africans] that's how it always has been) Our objective is for SELF SUFFICIENCY upon the land.

....
    Our objectives then are for:
    i) the collective scientifically and technologically based, and the 'imaginary resources' - that We have not yet started to really tap into as A Nation; and
    ii) the further safeguarding against the incursion of any forces which would deprive us of our hard-won

---

[52] The Ethiopia Jamaica Society (EJS) is presently been Incorporated.

liberty and dignity, by way of us been guided and inspired through the practice of the principle of COLLECTIVE SECURITY.

In short We are asking for the necessary tools of THE LAND, and the Continental (and international) support institutions to be put to Our disposal, so We can begin this timely indigenous process of Our own making: the re-claim, rebuilding and restoration of Ethiopia (Africa)...."

We would be amiss if We did not remind/enlighten Your Honorable Excellencies of the government sponsored 1961 Mission to Ethiopia and four other African States. The **"Majority Report"** and **"Minority Report"(s)**, [53] and the subsequent **"Technical Mission Report"** - that was never released to the public, members of the mission, and, or, Rastafari Community. [54]

---

[53] Ibid, **REPORT OF MISSION TO AFRICA.**

[54] See **"Interview between Everton Mc Pherson and Prof. Rex Nettleford, Mona Extra-Mural Department, Mona, University of the West Indies, Kingston, Jamaica, 1982;"** see also **"Letter from the RICWC to, Prof. Rex Nettleford, Extra-Mural Department, Mona, University of the West Indies, Kingston 7, 7.12.90;"** see also Bro. A. Foxe, "Nettleford 'no Rasta defender,'" **The Daily Gleaner** (Letter to the Editor), April 23, 1991, p. 7; see also Ras Everton Mc Pherson, Ilect of Throne - RICWC, **"Minutes from RICWC Elders and Executives meeting with Prof. Rex Nettleford on receiving, or the making of a Public declaration on 'the Technical Mission Report,'"** (Extra Mural Department, Mona, UWI, Kingston, Jamaica 10.12.90; see also Ras Everton Mc Pherson - Ilect of Throne - RICWC (Taped and Transcribed **"Preliminary Report by Ras Martimo Planno of the 1961 Mission; with a 1990 perspective,"** (given at the Ethiopian Orthodox Church, Maxfield Avenue, Kingston, 28 November 1990; given in the presence of Ras Everton Mc Pherson and Sis. Paula Shaw - Secretary of the RICWC).

Figure 33: Members of the Jamaican Back to Africa delegation with President Dr. Kwame Nkrumah, Accra Ghana, 1961; *standing* l-r: Munroe Scarlett, Mr. Victor Reid; Dr. Leslie; President Nkrumah; Bro. Douglas Mack; Bro. Martimo Planno, Hon. E. H. Lake, Minister of Social Welfare, Antigua; Bro. Philmore Alvaranga; and Ghanaian Protocol Chief; *sitting l-r:* Mr. Blackwood, the U. N. I. A. & A. C. L. Delegate; and Mr. Cecil Gordon, E. W. F., Inc. Rep.

The mission looked for "the possible movement of persons.. to settle," arrived in Addis Ababa Ethiopia, on Sunday April 16th, 1961. They visted "Sheshemani," the land the Emperor gave on September of 1955, [55] "for the people of African origin domiciled outside the continent and who desired to return." It should be keenly noted by Your Honorable Servants of Ethiopia, that when the mission was received by His Majesty on Friday April 21st, he welcomed Us as: **"brothers of one blood and race;"** and further asserted that: **"Ethiopia would always be open to people of African origin who lived in the West and who desired to return."** [56]

---

[55] See "George A. Bryan (Executive Secretary), Robert L. Johnson (International President), Maymie Richardson (International Organizer), 151 Lennox Avenue, New York 27, N.Y. September 24, 1955, Letter to the Executive Committee of Local No. 31 Ethiopian World Federation, Inc., 71 North Street, Kingston, Jamaica, B.W.I.," in ibid, M. G. Smith, Roy Augier, Rex Nettleford, **THE RASTAFARIAN MOVEMENT IN KINGSTON, JAMAICA,** Appendix VIII SOME CORRESPONDENCES., pp. 39-40. See **"Letter from the IMPERIAL ETHIOPIAN GOVERNMENT MINISTRY OF FOREIGN AFFAIRS, Addis Ababa, September 9th, 1959, to The Editor of The Gleaner, T. E. Sealy."**

[56] Ibid, **REPORT OF MISSION TO AFRICA,** p. 3.

Figure 34: [left] Nii Amo Nakwah II, the Obtobulum Mensah, Paramount Chief of the Ashanti praying for members of the Jamaican Back to Africa Delegation, in Accra Ghana 1961; Bro. Douglas Mack [center]

Figure 35: "Purification of stools and skins ceremony in Jamestown Accra (Dec '95) – Jah Blue & Ras Binghi."

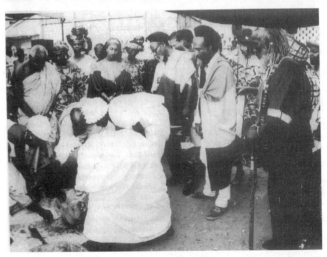

Figure 36: "The Land in Akwamu, given to black people of the diaspora – Ras Binghi & Jah Blue with Chiefs and Queen Mother."

Wisely noting that this "government mission" was an "unofficial" one, His Majesty said that We should: "send a delegation of experts from Jamaica to discuss the various facts of migration"/"send the right people." [57] This was one of the main reasons why the "Technical Mission" was sent by the said then Government-of-the-day. And this is why We have always considered that a public Report should be submitted by Prof.[s]. Rex Nettleford [Don Mill] et. al. [i. e. Aston Foreman; Wesley Miller], who were sent by the then Premier Norman Manley, Q.C.. [See Rex Nettleford, **Introduction: Fledging Years**, in Rex Nettleford (Edited), **Jamaica in independence Essays on the Early Years**, (Heinemann Caribbean, Kingston James Curry London), 1989, p. 9 footnote 11, pp. 331-332: In his words, The objective and result of *the Technical Mission* was, "to explore trading and formal cultural links.... A Jamaican Embassy was subsequently established in Addis Ababa."]

It is also noteworthy for Your Honorable Excellencies to remember that along with the land of Sheshemane given to

---

[57] Op. cit, pp. 3-4.

"the Peoples of the West," His Majesty further laid another basis for the reclaim of Our African/Ethiopian Sovereignty, that was to be the one of the integral component of the development of "dual citizenship." His Majesty was eager for exchanges of students and scholars between Ethiopia and the West Indies. This runs parallel to his earlier words at the last meeting of Independent African states held in Addis Ababa:

> "...We must see to it that the history of each other of our people is known to the others and appreciated throughout the continent." [58]

Thus, it must be evident to Your Excellencies why We need a restitution of the lands belonging to Us; and why a form of pro-active dual citizenship, would further integrate the Ethio-diaspora into the Ethiopian society, is necessary to be enshrined in this new constitution. Ethiopian Sovereignty as such would be transferred into the diaspora - to be the vanguard of this age in Our quest to realize A Single African Government. In this regard let Us remember the wise words, charge, and official commitment of one of Our Beloved Servants of Ethiopia, **Dr. Esin Esin**, the then Minister of State in the Ethiopian Government, at the time of the Mission. He said that:

> "...repatriation would be taken up by the Federal Government... Africa could easily absorb all the [then] three million people in the West Indies." [59]

It should be no surprise then, to Your Honorable Excellencies that the Report of this Mission to five African States (Nigeria, Ghana, Liberia, Sierra Leone, Ethiopia) **"Majority Report,"** prefaced its opening thus:

---

[58] Op. cit, p. 6.
[59] Op. cit, p. 18.

"The Mission found in all territories a ready acceptance of the principles of `repatriation of Africans living abroad, to the ancestral land,' as it was enunciated by the delegates of the Mission....

The Mission found a desire, in the territories visited, for three department of skilled immigrants: (a) Professional and technical, (b) Artisans, (c) Farmers.

The African hosts to the Mission all observed that persons entering Africa in any migration scheme should do so with the intention of becoming permanent residents in the country, and not as transients. The question pointed out, since special arrangements would be made in this connection..." [60]

Integral to the call for the restitution of the land and the repatriation quest is the current call for **REPARATIONS**. [61] For Us then, Repatriation with Reparations are key components relating to the question of the restitution/ reinstitution of THE LAND, that a newly created Constitution and **democratically elected Government-of-the-day** should address. Most fundamental to all of this is the mandatory reinstitution of ALL illegally seized property by the former government; and the protect and respect for individual property rights. [62]

---

[60] Op. cit, pp. 1-2.

[61] See Ras Everton Mc Pherson Co-Chairman, Ras Howard Gouldbourne Co-Chairman, Sis. Dawn White Treasurer, **"The Ethiopia Jamaica Society Letter to the OAU's Chairman and General Secretary"** (January 13th, 1992) that was dispatched by the Jamaican based Nigerian High Commissioner; a copy of which was delivered by the world renown tireless advocate, Heroine - **Queen Mother Moore** to The African Council of Elders, in the aftermath of Her leaving Jamaica on the 14th of January, 1992, in, **ETHIOPIA JAMAICA SOCIETY NEWSLETTER**, Vol. 1 No. 1 Black History Month Special, Feb.-Mar., 1992. In this historic letter there was a call for the immediate prioritization of the questions surrounding the NEED for The Restoration of the Solomonic Dynasty, The Liberation of Ethiopia; Repatriation with Reparations; and the resolve of the Azanian debacle in Southern Africa.

[62] See Getachew Mekasha, Ph.D., "ETHIOPIANS PROSPECTS A Possible Blueprint for the Future," **ETHIOPIAN REVIEW**, June 1991, p. 13, p. 14, p. 15.

Again for the records, We present that part of Our outlined AGENDA presented by the ENF to the TGE's representatives at the UN Permanent Mission:

5) The questions surrounding THE REINSTITUTION OF LANDS illegally seized by the Dergue, to the Peoples [63] - based on the pre August 1974 period, e. g. the EWF Shashamane Land Grant; [64] the EWF "Bale and

---

Dr. Mekasha, Chairman of Mo-Anbessa, from the earliest outset of the TGE's formation asserted that the TGE should declare null and void all the unjust laws and decrees enacted by the Derg since 1974.

[63] See Getachew Mekasha, Ph.D., "ETHIOPIANS PROSPECTS A Possible Blueprint for the Future," **ETHIOPIAN REVIEW**, June 1991, p.13, p. 14, p. 15: "...Only a return to traditional norms and values can bring a new revival of the national spirit and put Ethiopia firmly back on the road of true national salvation.

.....In any case, one of the first acts of a transitional administration will have to be declaring null and void all the unjust laws and decrees enacted by the Derg since 1974.

....A draft constitution must be prepared in advance for presentation and discussion among all groups participating in the formation of a new transitional government. Such a draft should particularly address the question of local autonomy and guarantee individual rights. Recommendations on these issues must be available to the population at large and to regional political groups so that they can serve to diffuse hostility among them..."

See also for example Hassan A. Sherif, Saudi Arabia , "Ye Dagnew Baraya is Better Than Ye Communist Baraya," **ETHIOPIAN REVIEW** (LETTER), February 1994, pp. 7-8: ."..The government's pledge for return to full democracy should not be limited to the liberalization of the press, public speaking or forming organization alone. These are truly the fundamentals of humans rights. However, the reinstitution of illegally seized property by the former government is equally as important for the victims to feel that the present government is not only different but also better. In return this may eventually trigger economic liberalization by installing confidence in citizens to be full participants in the stimulation efforts of the backward and devastated economy of the country....

For any democratic political party coming to power, the first priority must be to win back the confidence and trust of the people. One way to achieve this is to protect and respect individual property rights..."

[64] See A. R. King [Ras Tagass] Shashamane Development Officer (Prepared), **"ETHIOPIAN WORLD FEDERATION INC. DEVELOPMENT PROGRAMME FOR SHASHAMANE LAND - GRANT,"** (June/July 1990,: p. 4:

"...**Present Situation/Plight**
...**During the 1974 revolution many settlers after having land and possessions confiscated** became afraid and decided to leave Ethiopia....

Pre 1974 the land granted amounted to five hundred acres (five gasha). This amount had been settled on by around forty to fifty settlers. After the revolution the land-grant was **modified** and those settlers who remained were allocated 2.2 hectares for each family. A total of forty hectares was reserved for members of the E.W.F.. As stated in the government[']s letter addressed to the community in April of 1975, (see appendix). **However this amount was never allocated in full. In reality the settlers received only 11 hectares.... These lands being considered settler land has obviously led to fears that the remaining 11 hectares belonging to the settlers, now being encroached upon, will leave the[m].. with nothing to develop. Complaints have been made to the Governing authorities, namely the Municipality and the Ministry of Agriculture...**
C. Development Objective

Phases 2.3 and 4 of this project, which is the broader development goal **cannot be achieved unless the question of land is answered to.**
At this point what is required is:-

1. The government to come and view the present situation.
2. Decision to be made as to either;
   i. return back the original land-grant (500 acres)
   ii. grant addition land elsewhere.

The return of the original land-grant is more favored by the settlers as they are aware if their prime position either side of the main road and just 3 [kilometers] from the Shashamane town.

If addition land elsewhere were given most of the settlers would not give up their houses and immediate compounds to move elsewhere. Considering that some have been there twenty eight years and have grown various tree bearing fruits and other heavy lumber trees etc[.], this stance is understandable. (p. 16.)
.....**Associated History:- Revitalization of the Ethiopian [W]orld Federation**

...The help that the E.W.F. extended to the famine/drought [a]ffected victims opened up a new dialogue between the socialist democratic Government of Ethiopia and the E.W.F. both in England and Ethiopia. The P.S.C. [i. e. "Pioneer Settlers Corp"] made it known to the Government its desire to improve the situation and to develop the lands presently occupied..." [my emphases.]

See also "Jamaicans in Ethiopia laments of Embassy," **The Jamaica Record**, (n. d.): "**...Elaborating, Moody said the issue of the land granted to the EWF is still to be finalised and the Embassy has a vital role to play in assisting them in their negotiation with the new government..**" [my emphases.]; also in

Gobe Provinces" Grant; [65] and the Kennon Middle Eastern Corporation/Queen of Sheba and Pharaohs Masonic Movement [66] land grant. [[67]]

ETHIOPIA JAMAICA SOCIETY NEWSLETTER (DRAFT) Vol. 1 No. 1, which was edited and published Feb.-March 1992.
See also "Shock in Shashamane," in **The Jamaica Record**, (n. d.), op. cit):
"....Hail Majesty Haile Selassie I had granted us **200 hectares** of land in Shashamane. **When Mengistu came to power, we were given 40 hectares.** However we were in effective possession of **only 12 hectares.** Due to the efforts of the ambassador, the Mengistu regime had agreed to give us the full 40 hectares and the land was surveyed. We were on the verge of getting permission to fence it when the new government took control. At present, the Oromo people, who occupy the surrounding lands encroaching on us and want to take away the lands which were given to us by His Majesty and the Mengistu regime.
Many attempts were made to encroach on our lands over the past few years, but the ambassador was able to bring pressure on the officials in Addis Ababa who in turn pressured the local administration in Shashamane to respects pour right to the land grant...." [my emphases.]

See also B. J. Moodie, "An uncertain future in Ethiopia ," **The Jamaica Record**, November 17, 1991, p. 7A.

[65] See "LAND GRANT SECURED," **AFRICAN OPINION**, August-September, 1967, p. 5: "The Ethiopian World Federation, Inc. of Chicago reported a fund will be used for pioneering and developing 10,000 acres of Emperor Haile Selassie, of Ethiopia for Agricultural and other purposes.
The director, Rev. Winston G. Evans met His Imperial Majesty in Washington, D.C., February 13th and 14th, 1967 and requested the land which was subsequently granted....;" "LAND GRANT TO AFRICAN-AMERICANS," in **AFRICAN OPINION**, January-February, 1969, p. 9: "...Leaving Chicago by air in December, 1968, the couple visited Liberia, Senegal, Ghana and Ethiopia. In Accra, the Federation established registration and requested land for mutual development, the leaders reported.
The two representatives then departed for Ethiopia where the World Federation received 10,000 acres granted by His Majesty, Emperor Haile Selassie while he was on a visit to the United States in 1967..."

[66] See Robert Kennon, F.I.B.A. President Kennon Co., African & Middle Eastern, "Black Success Series Natural Allies To Revive Central Cities Passing Over Corporate Blacks," **The Observers Newspapers** [California], October 1-7, 1987, p. 5: "...This writer received a concession of **300,000 acres** for cattle culture and many industrial development options in partnership with various Ethiopian Rases (sub-Kings).

RETURN OF THE NATIONAL ANTHEM AND THE TOTEMIC LION FLAG: ROYALTY, BRAVERY and COURAGE

THE ENF DELEGATION to the TGE's U.N. Mission defended the rightful return of the totemic Lion in Our National Flag. We explained that this Ancestral emblem - the Lion, was A Symbol of the Royalty nature of Our Peoples, the Bravery and Courage of Our relentless and unconquerable Nation. Symbols, that historically transcend the reigning era of His Majesty's Government (1930-1974). Thus, since the Derg had rid itself of all of these national historical symbols relating to His Majesty's reign, the Flag been one of them, there should NOW be a return to civic pride and national sanity.

We, are here now also calling for the return of Our Ancient Ethiopian National Anthem. An Anthem that was wisely adopted by **The Rt. Hon. Marcus Garvey's UNIA**, which is another factor pointing to the Ethiopic cognitive appeal and identification within the diaspora and on the Continent, that

---

We has assembled a large number of American financiers and industrialist to develop Ethiopians through American capital when the communist revolution intervened in 1974...." [my emphases.]
See also in, **ETHIOPIA JAMAICA SOCIETY JOURNAL**, (forthcoming May, 1994).

[67] Ibid, **"THE ETHIOPIA JAMAICA SOCIETY - NEW YORK CHAPTER LED] MEETING BETWEEN THE ETHIOPIAN NATIONAL FRONT AND THE DEPUTY AMBASSADOR, MR. FIFFHA, OF THE PERMANENT MISSION OF ETHIOPIA TO THE UNITED NATIONS, ON THE 11TH OF APRIL, 1994, AT 866 UN PLAZA, NEW YORK, U.S.A. THE QUEST OF ETHIOPIAN SOVEREIGNTY: AFRICAN NATIONHOOD AGENDA,"** No. 5), pp. 4-6.

predated the Haile Selassie I era. That the greatest Black Organization of this century could have adopted the Ethiopian Anthem, is a very culturally meaningful signal - to Your Honorable Excellencies to re-consider and correct this further blunder of the Dergue's period of chaos.

The question Your Honorable Excellencies NEED to ask yourselves, was asked by **Abeba Fekade**, a contemporary Ethiopian psychologist Scholar whom We empathize with totally. He lamentably asked:

> "...Why for instance, the TPLF /EPLF have strong, almost pathological, drive for destruction of self and other Ethiopians by displaying resentment and offense toward Ethiopianess? **Why would a government ridicule or dislikes its national flag, and all other symbols of the Ethiopian nation...**" (p.65). (my emphases.) [68]

We have noted also a number of other Ethiopian based organizations that are also calling for the return of the Flag and the anthem, which Our case a non-sentimental one. For example, **The Ethiopian Chambers of Commerce** in their (already critiqued) document presented to the Commission said:

> "....the national flag should be given its appropriate place and Amharic should continue as the official language, without prejudice to the rights of the different nationalities to develop their own languages and cultures."

We are also in agreement with Amharic remaining the national language - with the right of all other Peoples to develop their own.

---

[68] See Abeba Fekade, "Miseducation: The Roots of the Current National Crisis," **Ethiopian Register** (Education/View Point/ Culture), July 1994, p. 65 (pp. 63-66).

We will end this section of Our Position Paper in a literary manner, that depicts the yearnings of Your kins in the diaspora.

Hear Our Voices in Jeannette F. Love's,

THE FALL AND RISE OF CUSHAN AND OTHER POEMS:

"Shall Ethiopia rise again
By the power of heaven 'twill rise,
For the mouth of God has spoken
And his words can never fail.
Through times mighty telescope,
See the nations of old,
Mustering in royal line;
Not unto the battle-drum
But to the gospel's silver chime.
Ethiopia's sons returned
....

> *Return the, Afric's sons return*
> *To the wide, wild waste beyond the sea;*
> *Country and kindred wait for thee*
> *Return ye from captivity.*

....

Return, ye loyal-hearted ones
And Africa no more shall be
The land of shadows, bit the clime
Sunny, of Ethiop's noble free...." [69]

---

[69] See Jeannette F. Love, **THE FALL AND RISE OF CUSHAN AND OTHER POEMS**, (The Stoneman Press Co., Columbus, Ohio), 1911, section called: **The Rise of Cushan**, pp. 23-24, 26.

CONCERNS:

1)

i) **N. B.: The 1993 Annual Country Report of the State Department**: "In contrast to the Mengistu years, the human rights situation in Ethiopia has improved. The TGE's actions did not match, however, its announced respect for human rights. In the face of opposition, it showed increasing intolerance of political dissent.," in Azeb Ze Mariam & Mikael Wossen,

"The Politics and Sophistry on Human Rights: Some Burning Questions," **Ethiopian Register**, April 1994, p.15.

ii) + p.18: "...the EDU is not permitted to open office in Tigray and candidates of the AAPO [/P] continued to be prevented from either registering many constituencies or holding public demonstrations, or they are simply harassed and arbitrarily detained (**Human Rights Watch Report** 1993) throughout the country. These and other well-documented curtailment of political rights, and the rising numbers of extra judicially imprisoned, silenced, tortured or executed citizens point to very dangerous trends in the country's alleged progress toward democratization..."

iii) + "The Council of Alternative Forces for Peace and Democracy (CAFPDE) in Ethiopia has also issued a press release on the prevailing situation. According to this press release CAFPDE and the independent newspapers, the principal targets of these terrorist acts are the members and suspected supporters of the All Amhara People's Organization (AAPO), the Ethiopian Democratic Union (EDU), Mo Anbessa, the National Democratic Union (NDU) and the Guragie People's Democratic Front (GPDF)...." [the victims are outlined, on pp. 15-16.]

iv) **N. B.:** "Mass Rally Against TPLF's 'Elections'" = the Council of Alternative Forces for Peace and Democracy in Ethiopia (CAFPDE), held in Addis Ababa's Meskel Square on April 16, 1994

v) **N. B.:** Getachew Mekasha, Ph.D., "ETHIOPIAN PROSPECTS A Possible Blueprint for the Future," **Ethiopia Review**, June 1991.

vi) **N. B.:** Getachew Haile, "EPRDF Should Be The Last Body To Draft Drafters Of A Constitution For Ethiopia," **Moresh**, April 1993, pp. 33-36.

vii) Girma Abebe, "ETHIOPIA: Strangulation by Staged Elections," **Ethiopian Register**, June 1994, pp. 30-37.

2) - Ethnocide/ethnic carving, ethno-politics; ethno-secessionists; Marxist Leninist/ Maoism - (Stalinism) revisionism

i) June 1992 elections mal-report and rape of democracy

ii) = the results of the June 5th Constituent assembly Elections

iii) - parties not in = "ENDP Won't Participate in the June Election," **Ethiopian Register** June 1994, pp. 13-14; "ENDP withdraws from constituent assembly elections," **The Ethiopian Herald**, 25 April 1994, p.6

iv) Parties banned by TGE = uneasy peace;

N. B.: "**Letter from Goshu Wolde, Chairman The Ethiopian Medhin Democratic Party, to The Inter-Africa Group, RE: RESPONSE TO AN INVITATION TO PARTICIPATION IN MENGISTU-STYLE 'CONSTITUTIONAL' PROCESS,**" (MEDHIN North American HQs, P.O. Box 9380, Washington, D.C. 20005), May 11, 1991

N. B.: "Interview With Col. Goshu Wolde Chairman of the Medhin Party," **ETHIOPIAN REVIEW**, December 1993, pp. 14-16; in **ETHIOPIA JAMAICA SOCIETY NEWSLETTER**, Vol. 1 No. 2 Black History Month Special: UNITY & DEVELOPMENT Feb.-Mar. 1994, pp. 12-15

+ "Interview with Colonel Goshu Wolde, Chairman of the Ethiopian Medhin Democratic Party," **Ethiopian Register**, May 1994, pp. 23-24.

+ See "**Ras Everton Mc Pherson Co-Chairman of the Ethiopia Jamaica Society (EJS); President of the Black International**

Iyahbinghi Press, Faxed-Letter to: Colonel Goshu Wolde Chairman, c/o Sieish Michael Zewbe, The Ethiopian Medhin Democratic Party (MEDHIN) North American Head Quarters, P.O. Box 9380, Washington, D.C. 20005, RE: FORMALIZATION OF EJS-MEDHIN WORKING AFFILIATION; QUESTIONS ON MOA-ANBESSA-MEDHIN RELATIONS; AND EJS REQUEST TO MEET MEDHIN'S CHAIR WITH AN ETHIO-DELEGATION, (August 2, 1993)."

3) = war by ESA:

i) [**N. B.: "MEDHIN's Annual Report,"** (1993): "MEDHIN's unavoidable resort to Arm-Struggle, after all political prospects and diplomatic efforts had been explored but had failed.."]

ii) "The Ethiopian Salvation Army Conducts Military Operations Against TPLF/EPRDF," **Ethiopian Register** (News in Brief), April 1994, pp. 9-10.

iii) "Ethiopian Salvation Army continues its Military Assault," **Ethiopian Register** (News in Brief), June 1994, pp. 8-9.

4) Party now in - AAPO now a Party

i) "AAPO becomes party to withstand systematic attacks: Prof. Asrat, **The Ethiopian Herald**, 22 April 1994, pp. 1 & 3.

"AAPO Transforms to a Political Organization," **Ethiopian Register** (News in Brief), May 1994, p. 8.

ii) Taye Assefa, "Interview with Professor Asrat Woldeyes, President of AAPO," **Ethiopian Register**, June 1994, pp. 16-24.

iii) "Prof. Asrat sentenced to two years imprisonment," **The Ethiopian Herald,** 28 June, 1994, p.1.

5) the most recent TGE Council of Rep. proclamation on leasing of urban lands:

Figure 37: Professor Asrat Woldeyes permitted to seek medical attention abroad.

i) **N. B.:** Anaclet Rwegayura, IPS, "Starve, But Ready For Polls," **THE AFRICAN OBSERVER**, May 31-June 13, 1994, p. 9. = TGE Council of Representatives Proclamation on lease holding of urban lands; U.S. Ambassador response; and OAU unseating from Africa's capital.

ii) "New Landlease Law Causes Anxiety," **Ethiopian Register**, June 1994, p.8.

iii) "Council Issues a New Land Lease Regulations for Addis Ababa," **Ethiopian Register**, June 1994, p.14.

6)

i) The comprehensive implementation of dual citizenship rights by diaspora government - e. g. n. b. **EJS Co-Chairman formal submission to the West Indian Commission, at the Webster Memorial Church, Half Way Tree Road, Kingston, Jamaica, on 20th February 1992**: "..that the questions of REPARATION and DUAL CITIZENSHIP be prioritized by CARICOM Heads, and be discussed with Our African Kins internationally and Continentally - in particularly with the OAU..."

In the preliminary Report put out by the Commission, there was no mention of any of these factors. We questioned the Jamaican Representative, Prof. Rex Nettleford on these matters, who informed Us that such was not deemed to be of such importance by the Commission. We lamented such shortsightedness of these Caribbean esteemed elite intellectuals.

ii) N. B.: Sheshamane Chamber of Commerce anti-dual citizenship views "Ethiopian Chamber of Commerce Proposes Constitutional Rights which Contradicts the EPRDF's Draft Constitution," **Ethiopian Register** (News Report), June 1994, p. 11

7) Lament of the role of the Ethio-diaspora/Revolutionary Ethiopianist Intellectual:

i) Dereje Alemayehu, "A Perspective for a Democratic Discourse," **Ethiopian Review** December 1993, pp. 31, subsection called: **The Responsibility of the Ethiopian Intelligentsia in the Diaspora**, p.31.

8) The move towards "constitutional rule" vs. "rule by default;" Ethiopia has to court consensus vs. misstep; vs. the impacting of our agenda - in our own way:

"Candidates' registration gathers momentum," **The Ethiopian Herald**, 22 April 1994, pp. 1 & 5.

"Malaysian king steps down," **The Ethiopian Herald**, 26 April 1994, p.3.

"ENDP withdraws from constituent assembly elections," **The Ethiopian Herald**, 25 April 1994, p.6.

"Council continue debate on draft constitution," **The Ethiopian Herald**, 24 April 1994, pp. 1 & 6.

Getachew Kejla (editor), "Secession and Constitution," **The Ethiopian Herald** (Constitutional Focus), 27 April 1994, p.8.

"Council continues discussion on draft constitution," **The Ethiopian Herald**, 26 April 1994, pp. 1 & 3.

"Islamic religion representatives present their views to be included in future constitution," **The Ethiopian Herald**, 24 March 1994, pp. 1 & 5.

"No separation if unity to be achieved on revolution: OPDO," **The Ethiopian Herald**, 24 March 1994, pp. 1 & 5.

"SUPREME LAW OF THE LAND (The Constitution)," (Prepared by Ethiopian National Federation S.C. Division, Post Office Box 2786, Fair Lawn, N. J. 07410 [USA]) (1994?/n.d.).

Resolutions: Leap Of Wisdom/ Conscious Evolution

RIGHTS: work, worship, media, judiciary, education, women, tourism, industry & commerce, ombudsman/justice

CHARGE:

- A "Constitutional Monarchy"
- A Imperial Federal Democratic Multi-Party State
- Return of the ancient national anthem and the totemic lion in the national flag
. Dual citizenship rights
. Ethio-Diaspora electoral franchise
- The reinstitution/restitution of the land
- Repatriation with Reparation
- Continental Federalism: A Single African Government.

Figure 38: Top "Haile Selassie I" [Salutes.]

Figure 39:Bottom: Afewerk Tekle, Ethiopia's leading artist [mural of H. I. M.]

Figure 40: [**H. I. M.** (Right) Honors the late Great Chief Warrior & Elder Statesman - **President Jomo Kenyatta** (Left) of Kenya.]

BIBLIOGRAPHY

" 'Assembly Sunday' - to form Party," **The Star**, February 7, 1961; also in ibid, Mc Pherson, **RASTAFARI and POLITICS...**, section called **Beginnings of A Modern Ethiopianist Emancipatory Movement: Bro. Sam Brown to Bro. 'Wally' Rodney**, p. 271; pp. 271-275.

Bey, Rahim Botswana (edited by Yusuf B. Tafari Bey), **I n I Self Law Am Master MOOR WISDOM**, (Rahim Bey), 1994.

Birhan, Farika (Public Relations Chairperson), **"PRESS RELEASE Ethiopian International Unification Committee (Jamaica),"** March 1987:

Bones, Jah, **One Love Rastafari: History, Doctrines & Livity**, (Voice of Rastafari Publishers), 1982.

Cashmore, Ernest, **Rastaman The Rastafarian Movement in England**, (George Allen & Unwin), 1979.

"CHAPTER VI LEGAL & CONSTITUTIONAL," subsection: PROMULGATING THE REVISED CONSTITUTION, in **SELECTED SPEECHES OF HIS IMPERIAL MAJESTY HAILE SELASSIE FIRST 1918 to 1967**, (The Imperial Ethiopian Ministry of Information Publication and Foreign Language Press Department, Addis Ababa, Ethiopia), 1967, p. 396.

Chevannes, Alston, Barry **Social and Ideological Origins of the Rastafari Movement in Jamaica**, (Submitted in partial fulfillment of the requirement for the degree Doctor of Philosophy under the executive Committee of the Graduate Schools of Arts and Science, Columbia University, 1989)

Diop, Cheikh Anta (translated by Harold J. Salemson), **BLACK AFRICA The Economic and Cultural Basis for a Federated State (with an interview by Carlos Moore)**, (Africa

World Press edition) 1974; new expanded revision 1987, pp. 15-16.

"ELECTION NEWS," [T.G.E. Election Commission, Addis Ababa, Ethiopia] (Received June 1994).

"Emperor's addresses both House of Parliament: Selassie stresses importance of co-operation between smaller states," **The Daily Gleaner**, April 22/23, 1966; also in: "HAILE SELASSIE ADDRESSES THE PEOPLE," **JAHMUG Centenary Edition**, (JAHMUG, P.O. Box 772, London SW11 5XY, 1991), pp. 6-7, 22; see also **ETHIOPIA JAMAICA SOCIETY NEWS- LETTER**, Vol. 1 No. 1 Black History Month Special Feb.-March 1992, p. 1; see also **"The reply of HIS IMPERIAL MAJESTY EMPEROR HAILE SELASSIE 1st. OF ETHIOPIA to Donald Sangster P.M. of Jamaica At the National Stadium, Kingston Jamaica. At the National Stadium, Kingston, Jamaica 21st April, 1966,"** (in, **E.I.U.C. Newsletter**, 133 Tower Street, Kingston, Jamaica, p. 1).

"Ethiopian Chamber of Commerce Proposes Constitutional Rights which Contradict the EPRDF's Draft Constitution," **Ethiopian Register,** June 1994, p. 11.

"ETHIOPIA JAMAICA SOCIETY FORMED PRESS RELEASE," December 23, 1991.

ETHIOPIA JAMAICA SOCIETY NEWSLETTER (DRAFT) Vol. 1 No. 1, which was edited and published Feb.-March 1992.

ETHIOPIA JAMAICA SOCIETY NEWS- LETTER, Vol. 1 No. 1 Black History Month Special Feb.-March 1992

ETHIOPIA JAMAICA SOCIETY JOURNAL, (forthcoming May, 1994).

Ethiopian Liberation Silver Jubilee 1941-1966, (Publication and Foreign Language Press Department, Ministry of Information, Addis Ababa - Ethiopia), 1966, pp. 121-122.

EJS Newsletter, Vol. 1 No. 1 Feb.-Mar., 1992, pp. 3.

"Ethiopian Salvation Army continues its Military Assault," **Ethiopian Register**, June 1994, pp. 8-9.

"EXCERPTS FROM THE CO-CHAIRMAN OF THE EJS & MO-ANBESSA, & ILECT OF THRONE OF THE NYAHBINGHI ORDER OF HIS MAJESTY RASTAFARI INTERNATIONAL COORDINATING WORKING COMMITTEE," (Saturday 14th March 1994).

Fekade, Abeba, "Miseducation: The Roots of the Current National Crisis," **Ethiopian Register** (Education/View Point/ Culture), July 1994, pp. 63-66.

Ford, Yosef, "**ETHIOPIA: IN SEARCH OF A NATIONAL IDENTITY Africans Cannot Liberate Themselves from,**" **Themselves**, (1993).

"Formation of Ethiopia-Jamaica [Society] Association," **The Weekend Star** (Positive Vibes), December 27, 1991, p. 4.

Foxe, A, **"The Rastafarians Past and Present,"** (A. Foxe, The Secretary, Jamaica Working Committee, Sub-Local 37, Ethiopian World Federation Inc., London W10,79 Chesterton Road), [pub./written early 1960s], in ibid, Mc Pherson, **RASTAFARI and POLITICS...**, p.261.

Foxe, Bro. A., Rasta participation in Jamaican politics," **The Daily Gleaner**, (Letter to the Editor), July 21, 1988, p. 6; in ibid, Mc Pherson, **RASTAFARI and POLITICS....**, p. 285, p. 295.

Foxe, Bro. A., "Nettleford 'no Rasta defender,'" **The Daily Gleaner** (Letter to the Editor), April 23, 1991, p. 7.

Garvey, Amy Jacques, & E. U. Essien-Udom eds., **More Philosophy and Opinions of Marcus Garvey Vols., 3 Previously Unpublished Papers**, (Frank Cass and Company Ltd.), 1977, p. 737

Garvey, Marcus (edited), **The Blackman**, Vol. 1, No. 6 Nov. 1934, p. 18; also in E.S.P. Mc Pherson B.A. (Hons.), **The Rt. Hon. "Marcus" Mosiah Garvey - The Black Moses & St. John The Divine; A Black Internationalist & "Philosophic Statesman's" Challenge to the State & Church, Educators & Our People. - A VOICE CRYING OUT IN THE WILDERNESS**, November 1980, pp. 15-16.

Garvey, The Rt. Hon. Marcus Mosiah, **"African Fundamentalism A Racial Hierarchy and Empire for Negroes NEGRO'S FAITH must be CONFIDENCE IN SELF His Creed: ONE GOD ONE AIM ONE DESTINY,"** p. 1.

"George A. Bryan (Executive Secretary), Robert L. Johnson (International President), Maymie Richardson (International Organizer), 151 Lennox Avenue, New York 27, N.Y. September 24, 1955, Letter to the Executive Committee of Local No. 31 Ethiopian World Federation, Inc., 71 North Street, Kingston, Jamaica, B.W.I.," in ibid, M. G. Smith, Roy Augier, Rex Nettleford, **THE RASTAFARIAN MOVEMENT IN KINGSTON, JAMAICA**, Appendix VIII SOME CORRESPONDENCES., pp. 39-40.

GENERAL ELECTION, in **IMPORTANT UTTERANCES OF H.I.M. EMPEROR HAILE SELASSIE I**, (Published by The Imperial Ministry of Information, Addis Ababa, Ethiopia) 1972, pp. 172, 173, 174.

Gouldbourne, Howard (Book Review), "Rastafari and Politics Pt. 1 & Pt. 11," **The Jamaica Record**, January 1992, p. 7; January 3, 1992, p. 7.

"HAILE SELASSIE ADDRESSES THE PEOPLE," **JAHMUG Centenary Edition**, (JAHMUG, P.O. Box 772, London SW11 5XY, 1991), pp. 6-7, 22

H. I. M.'s **"STATEMENT TO THE 1963 AFRICAN SUMMIT,"** May 23, 1963, in ibid, **UTTERANCES OF H.I.M...,** p. 364.

H. I. M.'s **"THRONE SPEECH [November 2] (1970,"** in **UTTERANCES..**, p. 245; also in Ras Everton/E.S.P. Mc Pherson, *"Rastafari, the Ethio-Diaspora and Ethiopia in this 'Age of Transition': The makings of A Pan-Ethiopianist Development March for Progress, Modernity and A Program-of-Action Towards the 21st century. A Paper presented at the First Rastafari/Ethiopian Cultural Celebration, on Saturday November 13, 1993, at International House, Philadelphia.,"* **ETHIOPIA JAMAICA SOCIETY NEWSLETTER**, Vol. 1 No. 2 Black History Month Special UNITY & DEVELOPMENT, Feb.-Mar. 1994, p. 22.

His Imperial Majesty's *radio broadcast, on the 5th of March 1974, calling for a "Draft Constitution,"* speech, dubbed: **"A GOVERNMENT DECLARATION OF GUIDANCE,"** in E.S.P. Mc Pherson, **RASTAFARI and POLITICS: Sixty Years of a Developing Cultural Ideology. A Sociology of Development Perspective**, pp. 55-59.

IMPORTANT UTTERANCES OF H.I.M. EMPEROR HAILE SELASSIE I, (Published by The Imperial Ministry of Information, Addis Ababa, Ethiopia), 1972.

"Interview between Everton Mc Pherson and Prof. Rex Nettleford, Mona Extra-Mural Department, Mona, University of the West Indies, Kingston, Jamaica, 1982."

"Jamaicans in Ethiopia laments of Embassy," **The Jamaica Record**, (n.d.)

Kennon, Robert F.I.B.A. President Kennon Co., African & Middle Eastern, "Black Success Series Natural Allies To Revive Central Cities Passing Over Corporate Blacks," **The Observers Newspapers** [California], October 1-7, 1987, p. 5

King, R. [Ras Tagass] Shashamane Development Officer (Prepared), **"ETHIOPIAN WORLD FEDERATION INC. DEVELOPMENT PROGRAMME FOR SHASHAMANE LAND - GRANT,"** (June/July 1990).

"LAND GRANT SECURED," **AFRICAN OPINION**, August-September, 1967, p. 5.

"LAND GRANT TO AFRICAN-AMERICANS," in **AFRICAN OPINION**, January-February, 1969, p. 9.

"**Letter from the IMPERIAL ETHIOPIAN GOVERNMENT MINISTRY OF FOREIGN AFFAIRS, Addis Ababa, September 9, 1959, to The Editor of The Gleaner, T. E. Sealy.**"

"**Letter from the RICWC to, Prof. Rex Nettleford, Extra-Mural Department, Mona, University of the West Indies, Kingston 7, 7.12.90**"

Love, Jeannette F., **THE FALL AND RISE OF CUSHAN AND OTHER POEMS**, (The Stoneman Press Co., Columbus, Ohio), 1911, especially the section called: **The Rise of Cushan**, on pp. 23,-24, 26.

Mc Donald, Steve, Steve, "**The Question of Race and the Concept of Liberation,**" (1987).

Mc Pherson, **The Rt. Hon. "Marcus" Mosiah Garvey - The Black Moses & St. John The Divine; A Black Internationalist & "Philosophic Statesman's" Challenge to the State & Church, Educators & Our People. - A VOICE CRYING OUT IN THE WILDERNESS**, (Frankfield P. O., Clarendon, Jamaica), November 1980.

Mc Pherson, E.S.P., **The Positive Relationship Between Religion and Cultural Development: A Case Study of Rastafari**, (A Sociology of Development M.Sc. Draft, Sociology Department, Mona, University of the West Indies, Kingston, Jamaica), 1988/9; 90-91.

Mc Pherson; Ras Everton: Ilect of Throne; Ilect of Records: Jasper Fertuado/Ras Ivi; Ilect of Treasury: Ras Irie Lion, "**A Summary Report of the National Rastafari Assembly Hosted by the Nyahbinghi Order of His Majesty Rastafari, held at the Social Welfare Center of the University** of the West Indies, Mona, Kingston, Jamaica, Saturday November 17th-Sunday 18th, 1990.," (The Nyahbinghi Order of His Majesty Rastafari International Coordinating Working Committee) [RICWC], c/o Ras Boanerges, Gold Smith Villa, Lot 215, Mona P.O., Kingston) November 1990; also in ibid, Mc Pherson, **RASTAFARI and POLITICS..**, pp. 198-199.

Mc Pherson, Ras Everton Ilect of Throne - RICWC, **"Minutes from RICWC Elders and Executives meeting with Prof. Rex Nettleford on receiving, or the making of a Public declaration on 'the Technical Mission Report,'"** (Extra Mural Department, Mona, UWI, Kingston, Jamaica 10.12.90.

Mc Pherson, Ras Everton - Ilect of Throne - RICWC (Taped and Transcribed), **"Preliminary Report by Ras Martimo Planno of the 1961 Mission; with a 1990 perspective,"** (given at the Ethiopian Orthodox Church, Maxfield Avenue, Kingston, 28 November 1990; given in the presence of Ras Everton Mc Pherson and Sis. Paula Shaw - Secretary of the RICWC).

Mc Pherson, E.S.P., **RASTAFARI and POLITICS: Sixty Years of a Developing Cultural Ideology. A Sociology of Development Perspective**, (Black International Iyahbinghi Press, Frankfield, Clarendon, Jamaica), September 2nd 1991

Mc Pherson, **RASTAFARI and POLITICS..**, Constitutional Monarchy "Laws of Succession," pp. 161-164.

Mc Pherson, **RASTAFARI and POLITICS.., CHAPTER 10 Towards the Beginnings of A New Ethiopia: The Restoration of the Solomonic Dynasty and "The Constitutional Monarchy,"** p.302; pp. 298-302.

Mc Pherson, Ras Everton Co-Chairman, Ras Howard Gouldbourne Co-Chairman, Sis. Dawn White Treasurer, **"The Ethiopia Jamaica Society Letter to the OAU's Chairman and**

General Secretary" (January 13th, 1992) that was dispatched by the Jamaican based Nigerian High Commissioner; a copy of which was delivered by the world renown tireless advocate, Heroine - **Queen Mother Moore** to The African Council of Elders, in the aftermath of Her leaving Jamaica on the 14th of January, 1992, in, **ETHIOPIA JAMAICA SOCIETY NEWS-LETTER**, Vol. 1 No. 1 Black History Month Special, Feb.-Mar., 1992.

Mc Pherson, Ras Everton Co-Chairman of The Ethiopia Jamaica Society; Co-Chairman of Mo-Anbessa Provisional Steering Committee, "**Letter To: His Imperial Highness/Majesty Of Ethiopia Emperor Amha Selassie I, Her Imperial Highness Empress Medferiah Work Of Ethiopia, His Imperial Highness Crown Prince Zera Yacob Amha Selassie I; c/o Bro. Dr. Getachew Mekasha, Private Secretary of His Imperial Majesty, [dated](September 4, 1992)**"

Mc Pherson, Ras Everton/E.S.P., "*Rastafari, the Ethio-Diaspora and Ethiopia in this 'Age of Transition': The makings of A Pan-Ethiopianist Development March for Progress, Modernity and A Program-of-Action Towards the 21st century. A Paper presented at the First Rastafari/Ethiopian Cultural Celebration, on Saturday November 13, 1993, at International House, Philadelphia.,*" **ETHIOPIA JAMAICA SOCIETY NEWS-LETTER**, Vol. 1 No. 2 Black History Month Special UNITY & DEVELOPMENT, Feb.-Mar. 1994, pp. 22-30.

Mc Pherson, E.S.P. B.A. (Hons.), "TIME OF JUBILEE AND RESTORATION," **GAFFAT ETHIOPIA** Amharic and English Monthly Newspaper, July 1993, Vol. 2 No. 3, pp. 1, 8, 11; also first published by **The Herald (Jamaica)** in a three part serialized feature: E.S.P. Mc Pherson, "A time of jubilee and restoration (Part One)," **The Herald**, August 16, 1992, p. 6A; see also: "RASTAFARI AND THE SE-

LASSIE CENTENARY..... The coming of the mystics (Second in a Series)," **The Herald**, August 17, 1992, pp. 6 & 7; see also: "RASTAFARI IN THE SELASSIE CENTENARY.... Jamaican perceptions and reality (Third in a series)," **The Herald**, August 19, 1992, p. 6.

Mc Pherson, "**ETHIOPIA: ONE NATION - MANY PEOPLES: E. J. S. & MO-ANBESSA decries the T. G. E./ E. P. R. D. F. (T. P. L. F. [M. L. L.]/ E. P. L. F. regime; THE DIASPORA CALLS FOR 'A REAL DEMOCRATIC CONSTITUENCY ASSEMBLY' CREATED CONSTITUTION & A PROGRAM-OF-ACTION. A Paper presented at a demonstration called by the Ethiopian Patriotic Organizations, at Teachers College, Columbia, New York, U. S. A., on Saturday, March 19, 1994.,**" (A Ethiopia Jamaica Society New York Chapter (EJSNY) Ethio-Rastaology Study Group Series, No. 4; BATTLE OF ADOWA CENTENARY CELEBRATION Work No. 9; E. N. F. Work # 1; "ORDER OF THE PRECEPTS"/Educational Program), March 19, 1994; reprinted October 1994; July 29, 1996; An E.N.F. – Education & Research, Arts & Science Foundation "OPEN-HOUSE BUILDING FUND" PROJECT PUBLICATION, August 1999..

Mc Pherson, Ras E.S.P. Founder Co-Chairman of the Ethiopia Jamaica Society - New York Chapter, Founder Chairman of the Ethiopian National Front (ENF) (Prepared), "**(THE ETHIOPIA JAMAICA SOCIETY LED) MEETING BETWEEN THE ETHIOPIAN NATIONAL FRONT AND THE DEPUTY AMBASSADOR, MR. FIFFHA, OF THE PERMANENT MISSION OF ETHIOPIA TO THE UNITED NATIONS, ON THE 11th OF APRIL, 1994, AT 866 UN PLAZA, NEW YORK, U.S.A. THE QUEST OF ETHIOPIAN SOVEREIGNTY: AFRICAN NATION-HOOD AGENDA**" (attachment).

"'MO-ANBESSA' THE CONQUERING LION A CALL TO RALLY ALL ETHIOPIAN,'" 1991.

"'MO-ANBESSA' THE CONQUERING LION Press Release," June 1991; also in ibid, Mc Pherson, **RASTAFARI and POLITICS...**, pp. 301-302.

Mekasha, Getachew Ph.D., "ETHIOPIANS PROSPECTS A Possible Blueprint for the Future," **ETHIOPIAN REVIEW**, June 1991, p.13, p. 14, p. 15.

Moodie, B. J., "An uncertain future in Ethiopia," **The Jamaica Record**, November 17, 1991, p. 7A.

"New Rastafarian group formed," **The Jamaica Record** (News), December 28th, 1991.

Norris, Katrin, **The Search for an Identity**, (Institute of Race Relations; London; Oxford University Press), 1962.

Planno, Mortimer, "West Indies Federation a Make-Shift," **African Opinion** (Letter to the Editor) July-August 1958.

Planno, Mortimer (Jamaica W. I.), "Repatriation - A Human's Right," **African Opinion**, Vol. 4 Mar.-April 1959 Nos. 11 & 12, pp. 6-7.

Planno, Martimo, "Back to Ethiopia," **The Daily Gleaner** (Letter to the Editor), January 15, 1962, pp. 6-7.

"Preamble to a summary proposal for constitutional change," **The Jamaica Record**, June 12, 1991, p. 7; also in ibid, Mc Pherson, **"Letter to H.I.M., H.I.M. & Crown Council of Ethiopia...,"** (September 4, 1992), **4. National Liberation and the Ethio-Jamaican Community.**, pp. 3-4

"Rastafarians in Jamaica and Britain," **NOTES & REPORTS Catholic Commission for Racial Justice**, No. 10 January 1982.

"REPORT OF MISSION TO AFRICA," (The Government Printer, Duke Street, Kingston), 1961.

"Report on the First International Rastafarian Conference held in Toronto, Ontario, Canada July 23rd-July 25th, 1982 'Unification of Rastafari,' 'Workshop NO. 4 RASTAFARI and education within the political and economic system,' Politics."

"RIGHT THE SECRETARIAT OF The United Ethiopian National Solidarity Supreme Council For the Freedom RIGHTS of the Ethiopian People to The Imperial Ethiopian Federal Democratic Government. PRESS RELEASE"/"The Message...," April 1989; also in, **OUR OWN** *The Pan Africanist Movement of Jamaica International Magazine*, Vol. 1 No. 1 March-June 1990, pp. 3-6; also in ibid, Mc Pherson, **RASTAFARI and POLITICS..**, pp. 180-188.

SELECTED SPEECHES OF HIS IMPERIAL MAJESTY HAILE SELASSIE FIRST 1918 to 1967, (The Imperial Ethiopian Ministry of Information Publication and Foreign Language Press Department, Addis Ababa, Ethiopia), 1967

Sherif, Hassan A. Saudi Arabia, "Ye Dagnew Baraya is Better Than Ye Communist Baraya," **ETHIOPIAN REVIEW** (LETTER), February 1994, pp. 7-8.

"Shock in Shashamane," in **The Jamaica Record**, (n. d.)

Smith, M. G., Roy Augier, Rex Nettleford, **THE RASTAFARIAN MOVEMENT IN KINGSTON, JAMAICA**, (ISER, University of the West Indies.), 1960; Appendix VIII SOME CORRESPONDENCES., pp. 39-40.

"STATE TERRORISM IS IN FULL SWING," **Ethiopian Register** (News Report), July 1994, pp. 15-16.

"STATEMENT BY HIS IMPERIAL MAJESTY AMHA SELASSIE I REGARDING THE OPPORTUNE SITUATION IN ETHIOPIA," 1991.

The Ethiopian Examiner, May 1993, p. 15.

"The Jamaica Progressive League Kingston, Jamaica Renewed," (1989).

"The reply of HIS IMPERIAL MAJESTY EMPEROR HAILE SELASSIE 1st. OF ETHIOPIA to Donald Sangster P.M. of Jamaica At the National Stadium, Kingston Jamaica. At the National Stadium, Kingston, Jamaica 21st April, 1966," (in, **E.I.U.C. Newsletter**, 133 Tower Street, Kingston, Jamaica, p. 1).

"'10. Speech Delivered by Marcus Garvey on the steps of Ward Theatre, Kingston, Jamaica'" (from **The Blackman**, March 29, 1930), in ibid, Amy Jacques Garvey & E.U. Essien-Udom eds., **More Philosophy and Opinions of Marcus Garvey Vols., 3 Previously Unpublished Papers**, p. 737; also in ibid, Mc Pherson, **RASTAFARI and POLITICS.., CHAPTER 9 The Politics of Liberation: Theocracy - a Developing Cultural Ideology, subsection called: Rastafari: A science of Government: A Theistic Ideology**, p. 261; pp. 261-297.

Tafari, Ikael, **RASTAFARI and the GRENADA REVOLUTION: From Cultural Resistance to Political Liberation Completing the Second Cycle**, (Unpublished Paper, Cave Hill, University of the West Indies, Barbados), 1992.

The Bible, (King James Version).

The Daily Gleaner, Jan. 15, 1962, p. 8.

"The Ethiopian Salvation Army Conducts Military Operations Against TPLF/EPRDF," **Ethiopian Register**, April 1994, pp. 9-10.

The Royal Ethiopian Judah Coptic Church political manifesto, entitled, **"The Ethiopian-African Theocracy Union Policy (EATUP) True Genuine Authentic Policy: (FIOCAP),"** 1984; also in, Mc Pherson, **RASTAFARI..**, p. 289; see also ibid, Mc Pherson, **RASTAFARI and POLITICS..,** Chapter 9, section called **EATUP: The Royal Ethiopian Judah Coptic Church 1984-1988**, pp. 288-290; see also ibid, Alston Barry Chevannes, **Social and Ideological Origins of the Rastafari Movement in Jamaica**, pp. 414-416.

"**TOWN MEETING on THE CURRENT SITUATION IN ETHIOPIA With Emphasis on the Ethiopian Academic Community and Human Rights Violations Guest Speakers: Among the Illegally Dismissed Addis Ababa University Faculty Members . Professor Solomon Terfa Former Head, Political Science Department . Professor Meskerem Abebe, 1-5 p.m., Sunday, JULY 25, 1993, Horace Mann Hall at Teachers College, Columbia University, New York, NY.**" See also "**AN ETHIOPIAN TOWN MEETING at Columbia University Co-sponsored By THE AFRICAN STUDENTS ASSOCIATION AND MEDHIN. `The Current Situation in Ethiopia with Emphasis on Peace, Democracy, and Human Rights Violations By Col. Goshu Wolde Chairman of Medhin.,'** Saturday, August 7, 1993, Columbia University, Teachers College, Horace Mann Hall."

"**URGENT CALL TO SAVE ETHIOPIA FROM DISINTEGRATION AND ETHNIC DICTATOR-SHIP! YESTERDAY YUGOSLAVIA AND SOMALIA, TODAY IT IS RWANDA, AND TOMORROW IT MIGHT BE OUR OWN ETHIOPIA!,**" (A Paper put out by The Coordinating Committee of the Ethiopian Opposition Forces; published by MEDHIN, North American H.Q., Washington, D.C. 20005, U.S.A.), August 9, 1994.

"What we seek for Africa The Words of His Imperial Majesty Haile Selassie of Ethiopia," **Reggae & Africa Beat**, Vol.8 #1 1989, p.7; in ibid, Mc Pherson, **RASTAFARI...**, p. 2.

Williams, Dr. Chancellor (introduction by Baba El Senzengakulu Zulu Founder & Director of Ujamaa School), **THE RE-**

BIRTH OF AFRICAN CIVILIZATION, (U.B. & U.S. COMMUNICATIONS SYSTEM, INC.), 1993.

∧∧∧∧∧∧∧

ETHIOPIAN NATIONAL FRONT - (ENF EDUCATION AND RESEARCH, ARTS AND SCIENCE FOUNDATION CATALOGUE

- "BROTHER BEDWARD," (Jamaica, March, 1984).
- "BROTHER BEDWARD - A Reason Presented By E.S.P. Mc Pherson B.A. (Hons.) (U.W.I.), at the Chapleton & District Historical Society - Public Meeting, Thursday 24th of May, 1984, 7.00 p.m., at Salem United Church, Chapleton, Clarendon, Jamaica," (Jamaica March 1985).
- A MESSAGE OF HOPE AND DELIVERANCE - To Grassroots People in Jamaica (and the Caribbean), (USA, September 1993).
- "...RASTAFARI: TOWARDS PAN-ETHIOPIANIZATION (SOVEREIGNTY) AND A SINGLE CONTINENTAL GOVERNMENT (NATIONHOOD) *(A Paper Presented to the Secretariat of the 7th Pan Africanist Congress, held in Kampala, Uganda, Africa, April 4th, 1994)."*
- ALL L.I.O.N. (LIBERTY IN OUR NATION) WILL RETURN: A CONTINENTAL FEDERAL FORMULA, *(A Speech Presented to the Borough of Manhattan Community College/BMCC Student Government, at the Black Solidarity Day Celebration; THEME: "Unity Among the Family, Community, and Nation," held on November 3, 1997).*
- RASTAFARI/RASTAOLOGY: CULTURE, IDEOLOGY, POWER, & KNOWLEDGE. Towards the Development of "The New Education" (/an 'African-American') Curricula *(A Paper Presented to The Board of Education Title One Committee,*

Hyatt Hotel, Brunswick, New Jeresy, New York City, U. S. A., Saturday June 6th, 1998).

- THE ETHIO-DIASPORA CRY! THE ETHIOPIAN NATIONAL FRONT (ENF) & MOA-ANBESSA (THE CONQUERING LION ORGANIZING COMMITTEE) CHARGES: ETHNOCIDE IN, & DISINTEGRATION OF, ETHIOPIA (AFRICA)..., (USA, November 6, 1998).
- FROM ADDIS ABABA TO HARLEM: An Ethio-Rastafari International Perspective of The Million Youth March/M.Y.M., (USA, July 17-19,1998-September 3, 1998, THE DAILY CHALLENGE; released September 5th, 1999).

Forthcoming Publications

- ETHIOPIA SHALL BE REDEEMED: And Her Rightful Heir Shall Sit Upon Her Throne; THE RESURRECTION OF THE ETHIOPIAN QUESTION - in another political phase of action.
- ETHIOPIC NEWS WATCH JOURNAL, Vol. 1 No. 1.
- From "THE BLACK CHURCHES..." - BOOK TWO

Cassettes

- RASTAFARI & RASTAOLOGY: *The Meeting at 'The African Village Square'*, An Interview between **Bro. Junior Jawara Blake**, *Host of* "The African Village Square," on *Caribbean Entertainment Network/CEN, WRTN Radio Station*, New Rochelle, New York, USA, and **Ras E.S.P. Mc Pherson...**, (Sunday 5th, 1996; released March 1998).

Distribution Price: ....$ 6.50
Retail: ....$10 .00

- **...to begin the Reclamation of Our Ethiopian Sovereignty Tapes 1 & 2**, *An Interview between* **Ras Negus Dawit ['David']**, *Host of* **"Reggae Vibrations,"** and **Ras E.S.P. Mc Pherson...**, on **WHCR/Harlem Community Radio 90.3 FM**, 9 p.m.-12 p.m., City College, Harlem, New York, USA, Wednesday June 17, 1997 (; released June 1998).

DISTRIBUTION PRICE: ....$ 6.50
RETAIL: $10.00

∧∧∧∧∧∧∧

WRITE TO: Ras E.S.P. Mc Pherson,
Ethiopian National Front - (ENF)
Education & Research, Arts & Science Foundation,
c/o, 2507 Holland Avenue,
Bronx, New York, 10467,
U.S.A.
Phone: 1-212-368-5651; or: 1-917-362-5493
E-MAIL: kumina@tbol.net
WEBSITE:
http://members.tripod.com/~rastaology

RAS E.S.P. MC PHERSON
Published & Distributed by
A&B Publishers Group

* THE PROMISED KEY.
* From "THE BLACK CHURCHES...:" A Historiographic Taxonomy of Religion in Jamaica book one.
* RASTAFARI AND POLITICS: Sixty Years of a Developing Cultural Ideology. A Sociology of Development Perspective.
* ETHIOPIA: ONE NATION - MANY PEOPLES...
* THE ROLE OF THE REVOLUTIONARY ETHIOPIANIST INTELLECTUAL: Prescriptives for a Paradigm-Shift Towards "The New Education" (inclusive of RASTAOLOGY).
* THE CULTURE-HISTORY & UNIVERSAL SPREAD OF RASTAFARI: Two Essays.
* RASTAFARI: The People's Theology from *'Below'* Hermeneutic Interpretation; An Open Challenge to *'The Church'*
* RASTAFARI & RASTAOLOGY: *The Meeting at "The African Village Square"* An Interview...
* ETHIOPIAN SOVEREIGNTY: AFRICAN NATIONHOOD: Voices from The Ethio-Diaspora Call...
* TEACH THE WAY FORWARD: Chant from 'De Irit' [The Spirit]: "The New Education" and Information-Age.

∧∧∧

INDEX

A

a neo-traditional wing of the Ancient Nyahbinghi Order of His Majesty, 8
a renewed constitution, 4
A Single African Government, 71, 86
A. R. King [Ras Tagass] Shashamane Development Officer, 74
affirmative action
    affirmative collective action, 5
    collective actions, 26
Africa, 3, 4, 5, 6, 25, 26, 27, 28, 29, 30, 31, 32, 48, 52, 53, 58, 66, 71, 72, 79, 83, 90, 102, 103
AFRICA 2000, 5, 28
Africa, at home and abroad, 25
African, 3, 5, 25, 28, 30, 31, 32, 50, 53, 66, 68, 71, 72, 76, 84, 86, 92, 93, 96, 98
    African states, 71
    Africans, 4, 6, 26, 29, 30, 50, 57, 59, 65, 72, 91
    Azanian debacle in Southern Africa, 72
African Nationhood, 3
    An African Development Programme, 30
    Ethiopianess, 25, 57, 78
African states, 71
All Amhara People's Organization (AAPO), 80
alternative development strategizing method, 6
Amharic, 17, 56, 58, 78, 97
An African Development Programme, 30
anti-dual citizenship, 19, 84
Artisans, 72
Azanian debacle in Southern Africa, 72

B

Bey, Rahim Botswana, 89

C

Caribbean, 103, 104
Ceremonial Federalism, 43
Chairman of the Pan Africanist Movement Constitutional Committee, 16
Churches
    The Church, 106
    The Spirit, 106
Civil Guardian, 5, 46
Col. Goshu Wolde, 48, 81, 101
Columbia University, 12, 17, 47, 48, 49, 55, 89, 101
Community:, 103, 105
Constituent Assembly, 3, 17, 28, 33, 44, 54
Constitution Day, June 16th, 1931, 21
Constitutional exercise, 17
Constitutional Law
    Constitutional Rights, 19, 84, 90
    Democracy, 5, 48, 80, 101
    Multi-Party Democracy, 5
    Parliament, 13, 32, 33, 41, 42, 58, 59, 90
    the State, 21, 22, 43, 80, 92, 94

Constitutional Monarchy, 5, 10, 13, 32, 33, 40, 41, 43, 45, 49, 86, 95, 96
   a renewed constitution, 4
   Civil Guardian, 5, 46
   Emperor Amha Selassie I, 41, 96
   Good Government, 24
   H.I.H. Amha Selassie, 5, 40, 41, 44
   H.I.M. Amha Selassie I, 36, 40, 43
   Her Imperial Highness Empress Medferiah Work Of Ethiopia, 41, 96
   His Imperial Highness Crown Prince Zera Yacob Amha Selassie I, 41, 96
   Restoration Program, 11
   The Crown Council of Ethiopia, 40
   The Monarchy, 13, 41, 43
   The Royal Family of Ethiopia, 11, 40
Constitutional Rights, 19, 84, 90
cultural differences, 56

D

Democracy, 5, 48, 80, 101
Derg, 73, 77
   the Ministry of Agriculture, 74
Dictionary, 58
Draft Constitution, 1, 5, 12, 13, 19, 84, 90, 93
Dual Citizenship
   anti-dual citizenship, 19, 84

E

EATUP Manifesto, 8, 48
Education, 78, 91, 97, 103, 105, 106
   City College, 105
   Educational Program, 97
EJS Co-Chair, 15, 84
EJSNY, iv, 2, 65, 97
Emperor Amha Selassie I, 41, 96
ENF, iv, 1, 3, 4, 6, 8, 14, 15, 16, 17, 32, 40, 46, 47, 50, 56, 57, 64, 65, 73, 77, 97, 103
EPRDF, 12, 17, 19, 81, 82, 84, 90, 100
   Constituent Assembly, 3, 4, 17, 28, 33, 44, 54
   The Constitution Commission, 17
   The Permanent Mission Of Ethiopia To The United Nations, 13, 16, 76, 98
   The Transitional Government of Ethiopia, 17
   TPLF, 12, 19, 78, 80, 82, 100
Eritrea, 13, 64
ESA, 19, 82
Ethio-Americans, 4
Ethio-Americas, 46, 50
Ethio-Diaspora, 3, 25, 43, 47, 86, 93, 96
Ethio-diaspora Community, 21
Ethio-Jamaicans, 4
Ethiopia, iv, 1, 2, 3, 4, 5, 6, 10, 11, 12, 13, 14, 15, 17, 19, 21, 24, 25, 26, 27, 28, 29, 30, 32, 33, 36, 40, 41, 42, 43, 44, 45, 46, 47, 48, 49, 50, 52, 53, 55, 56, 57, 58, 59, 64, 65, 66, 68, 71, 72, 73, 74, 75, 76, 78, 79, 80, 81, 82, 84, 89, 90, 92, 93, 95, 96, 97, 98, 99, 101, 102
   Ethiopian Nation, iv, 3, 4, 21, 43, 54, 77, 85, 97, 99
   Ethiopian National Anthem, 77

Ethiopians, 4, 6, 21, 24, 25, 26, 30, 43, 48, 50, 54, 58, 65, 76, 78
Ethiopia Jamaica Society - New York Chapter, 97
EJS, 3, 4, 8, 11, 12, 13, 14, 15, 16, 47, 48, 49, 65, 82, 84, 91
EJSNY, iv, 2, 97
Ethiopia Jamaica Society - New York Chapter, 97
The African Council of Elders, 72, 96
the OAU's Chairman, 72
Ethiopia Jamaica Society (EJS), 3, 65, 82
Ethiopian based organizations, 78
Ethiopian Salvation Army, 19, 82, 91, 100
Ethiopian Nation, iv, 1, 3, 4, 21, 43, 54, 77, 85, 97, 99
Ethiopian National Anthem, 77
Ethiopian National Front, iv, 1, 3, 4, 97
Education & Research, Arts & Science Foundation, 105
ENF, iv, 1, 3, 4, 6, 8, 14, 15, 16, 17, 32, 40, 46, 47, 50, 56, 57, 64, 73, 77, 97
Ethiopian National Front, iv, 3, 4, 97, 105
Ethiopian National Front - New York
ENF, 103, 104, 105
Ethiopian National Front (ENF), iv, 3
Ethiopian Patriotic Organizations, 12, 47, 97
Ethiopian Salvation Army, 19, 82, 91, 100

Ethiopian Sovereignty, 3, 25, 46, 71
Ethiopian World Federation, Inc., 51, 68, 75, 92
Shashamane Development Officer, 74
Ethiopian World Federation, Inc., 51, 68, 75, 92
EWF, 8, 14, 51, 64, 74, 75
Ethiopianess, 25, 57, 78
Ethiopians, 4, 6, 21, 24, 25, 26, 30, 43, 48, 50, 54, 58, 65, 76, 78
Ethiopic, 77
ethno-linguistics, 56
ethno-linguistics, 56
EWF, 8, 14, 51, 64, 74, 75

F

Farmers, 72
Federalism, 43, 86
Ford, Yosef, 91
Founder-Chairman of the Lion of Judah Society, 16

G

Gabriel 'Blue' Adams, 51
Garvey, The Rt. Hon. Marcus Mosiah, 92
George A. Bryan (Executive Secretary), 68
Ghana, 72, 76
Good Government, 24
Gouldbourne, Howard, 92

H

H.I.H. Amha Selassie, 5, 40, 41, 44
H.I.M. Amha Selassie I, 40, 43
Her Imperial Highness Empress Medferiah Work Of Ethiopia, 41, 96

His Imperial Highness Crown Prince Zera Yacob Amha Selassie I, 41, 96

I

Ilect of Record, 10, 95
Ilect of Throne, 10, 12, 66, 95
Ilect of Treasury, 10, 95
Independent African states, 71
International President of the Imperial Ethiopian World Federation, Inc. (IEWF), 51

J

Jamaica, iv, 1, 2, 3, 5, 8, 10, 11, 14, 16, 22, 40, 41, 43, 48, 49, 50, 51, 52, 53, 54, 58, 59, 65, 66, 68, 70, 72, 75, 82, 84, 89, 90, 91, 92, 93, 94, 95, 96, 97, 98, 99, 100, 101

Chapleton, 103

Clarendon, 103

Jamaica, 103, 106

Jamaica Progressive League, 8, 14, 49, 100

JPL, 8

Jamaicans, 49, 58, 59, 75, 93

JPL, 8

K

Kampala, Uganda, 16

L

Letter From The Imperial Ethiopian Government Ministry Of Foreign Affairs, 68, 94
Letter from the RICWC to, Prof. Rex Nettleford, 66, 94
Liberia, 72, 76

M

Majority Report, 66, 72
Marcus Garvey, 22, 77, 91, 100

Africa, at home and abroad, 25

Maymie Richardson (International Organizer), 68, 92
Mc Pherson, E.S.P.

Ethiopian National Front, 105

Ras E.S.P., 104, 105

Mc Pherson, Ras E.S.P., 97

Education & Research, Arts & Science Foundation, 105

ENF, 103, 104, 105

Ilect of Throne, 10, 12, 66, 95

Negusa Nagast, 16

MEDHIN, 17, 19, 48, 81, 82, 101
Michael Zewbe, 82
Minority Report, 66
Moa-Anbessa, 8, 12, 14, 15, 16, 43, 47, 48, 49
Multi-Party Democracy, 5

N

Nationality, 55, 58
Nationality (Originality), 58
Nationhood, 3
Negusa Nagast, 16
neo-Garveyite, 51
New York Chapter, iv, 2, 3, 4, 16
Nigeria, 72

O

Office, 20, 85
organization, 29, 31, 41, 43, 44, 73

organization Ethiopian based organizations, 78

organization the Ethiopian Patriotic Organization, 12, 47, 97

The Coordinating Committee of the Ethiopian Opposition Forces, 17, 101
Our Beloved Honorable Ancestor, Saint and Elder, 22
Our Homeland, 59

P

Pan-Africanist, 25, 59
Pan-Ethiopianization, 26, 31
Parliament, 13, 32, 33, 41, 42, 58, 59, 90
permanent headquarters, 27, 29
Prof. Asrat sentenced, 82
Prof. Asrat sentenced All Amhara People's Organization (AAPO):, 82
PROJECT, 97
Psalm 137 verse 1, 3
Public, 17, 32, 40, 55, 66, 89, 95

R

Ras Everton, 10, 12, 15, 16, 25, 41, 47, 66, 72, 82, 93, 95, 96
Rastafari, 4, 8, 10, 12, 13, 14, 22, 25, 46, 48, 49, 50, 51, 52, 53, 59, 66, 89, 92, 93, 94, 95, 96, 99, 100, 101

Ethio-Rastafari, 104
Rastafari International Community, 4
Reparations, 20, 72
Repatriation, 20, 28, 50, 65, 72, 86, 98
Repatriation with Reparations, 72
Report Of Mission To Africa, 58, 66, 68, 99

Artisans, 72

Farmers, 72

Report Of Mission To Africa Majority Report, 66, 72

Report Of Mission To Africa Minority Report, 66
Restoration Program, 11
RICWC, 11, 13, 66, 94, 95

Ilect of Record, 10, 95

Ilect of Throne, 10, 12, 66, 95

Ilect of Treasury, 10, 95

Letter from the RICWC to, Prof. Rex Nettleford, 66, 94

RICWC:, 11, 13, 66, 94, 95

Summary Resolution, 10
Robert L. Johnson (International President), 68, 92

S

Saudi Arabia, 73, 99
secessionist act, 13
Selassie I, His Majesty Haile:, 68, 94
Shashamane, 59, 74, 75, 94, 99
Sherif, Hassan A., 99
Sheshamane Chamber of Commerce, 84
Sheshemani, 68
Sierra Leone, 72
Smith, M. G., 99
Southern Africa, 72
Sovereignty, 3, 4, 24, 25, 30, 46, 48, 54, 58, 71

Sovereignty, 105
Spirit, 106
St. Luke 15 verses 11-32, 3
Summary Resolution, 10
Symbol, 43, 77

T

Taxonomy, 106
TGE, 4, 12, 13, 14, 15, 17, 19, 32, 33, 44, 55, 73, 77, 80, 81, 83
The African Council of Elders, 72, 96

The Bible, 3, 25, 100
   David, 105
   St. Luke 15 verses 11-32, 3
The Blackman, 22, 92, 100
The Church of Haile Selassie I, 51
   International President of the Imperial Ethiopian World Federation, Inc. (IEWF), 51
The Coordinating Committee of the Ethiopian Opposition Forces, 17, 101
The Crown Council of Ethiopia, 40
The Deeperlite Spiritual and Cultural Liberation Theological Assembly, 14
the Deeperlite Spiritual and Cultural Liberation Theological Assembly Movement, 8
the ENF constituencies, 64
the Ethiopian Patriotic Organization, 12, 47, 97
The Ethiopian World Federation, Inc., 75
   A. R. King [Ras Tagass] Shashamane Development Officer, 74
   EWF, 8, 14, 51, 64, 74, 75
   Gabriel 'Blue' Adams, 51
   Maymie Richardson (International Organizer), 68, 92
   Robert L. Johnson (International President), 68, 92
   Shashamane, 59, 74, 75, 94, 99
   Sheshemani, 68

The Ethiopian World Federation, Inc., 75
   the Ministry of Agriculture, 74
The Haile Selassie Theocracy Governmant of His Majesty Haile Selassie I, 8
the June 5th Constituent Assembly Election results, 17
The Lion of Judah Society
   Founder-Chairman of the Lion of Judah Society, 16
the Ministry of Agriculture, 74
The Monarchy, 13, 41, 43
the OAU, 27, 28, 29, 59, 65, 72, 84
the OAU Charter, 59
The Royal Ethiopian Judah Coptic Church, 48, 101
   EATUP Manifesto, 8, 48
The Royal Family of Ethiopia, 11, 40
the State, 21, 22, 43, 80, 92, 94
The Transitional Government of Ethiopia, 17
the Universal Black Improvement Organisation (UBIO)
   neo-Garveyite, 51
Third World peoples, 57
TPLF, 12, 19, 78, 80, 82, 100

U

unification of Ethiopia (and Africa), 4
Universal Ethiopianess, 25
   USA, 103, 104, 105

Z

Zagwe Dynasty, 59

A&B Publishers Group
Send for our complete full color catalog today!

Title	Author	Price
*A Taste of the African Table	Blessing Egwu	(19.95) 11.95
A Book of The Beginnings Vol. I & II	Massey	45.00
Afrikan Holistic Health	Afrika	14.95
African Discovery of America	Weiner	10.00
*Arab Invasion of Egypt & The First 30 Years of Roman Dominion		(22.95) 15.95
Anacalypsis (set)	Massey	45.00
Anacalypsis Vol. I	Massey	25.00
Anacalypsis Vol. II	Massey	20.00
Aids The End of Civilization	Douglass	9.95
*Aquarian Gospel of Jesus the Christ	Levi	(19.95) 14.95
Black Heroes of The Martial Arts	Van Clief	16.95
*Apocrypha (hc)		14.95
British Historians & The West Indies	Eric Williams	9.95
Christopher Columbus & The African Holocaust	John Henrik Clarke	10.00
Columbus Conspiracy	Bradley	11.95
Dawn Voyage: The Black African Discovery of America	Bradley	11.95
Documents of West Indian History	Eric Williams	9.95
*Education of The Negro	Carter G. Woodson	(19.95) 10.95
*Egyptian Book of The Dead	Budge	(19.95) 11.95
Egyptian Book of The Dead/Ancient Mysteries of Amenta	Massey	9.95
*Enoch the Ethiopian Lost prophet of the Bible	Cush	(21.95) 14.95
First Council of Nice: A World's Christian Convention A.D. 325		9.95
Forbidden Books of The New Testament		14.95
*Gerald Massey's Lectures		(19.95) 9.95
Global Afrikan Presence	Edward Scobie	14.95
Gospel of Barnabas		11.95
Greater Key of Solomon		10.00
Hairlocking: Everything You Need To Know	Nekhena Evans	9.95
Harlem Voices from the Soul of Black America	John Henrik Clarke	11.95
Harlem USA	John Henrik Clarke	11.95
Healthy Foods & Spiritual Nutrition Handbook	Keith Wright	8.95
*Heal Thyself for Health and Longevity	Queen Afua	(19.95) 12.95
Heal Thyself Cookbook: Holistic Cooking with Juices	Diane Ciccone	10.95
Historical Jesus & the Mythical Christ	Gerald Massey	9.95
History of The People of Trinidad & Tobago	Eric Williams	14.95
*Lost Books of The Bible & The Forgotten Books of Eden		(21.95) 11.95
Oludumare: God In Yoruba Belief		12.95
Rape of Paradise: Columbus and the Birth of Racism in America	Carew	14.95
*Signs & Symbols of Primordial man		(25.95) 16.95
Vaccines are Dangerous: A Warning To The Black Community		9.95
Vitamins & Minerals A to Z	Jewel Pookrum	9.95
What They Never Told You In History Class Vol. 1	Khamit Cush	16.95
*Freemasonry An Interpreted		12.95
*Freemasonry & The Vatican		11.95
*Freemasonry & Judaism		11.95
Freemasonry: Character & Claims		9.95
Freemasonry: Exposition & Illustrations of Freemasonry		9.95
Science of Melanin		12.95
*Secret Societies & Subversive Movements		12.95

*(Hc pricing) Also available in hard cover   Prices subject to change without notice

---

Mail To: **A&B PUBLISHERS GROUP · 1000 ATLANTIC AVE · NEW YORK · 11238**
TEL: (718) 783-7808 · FAX (718) 783-7267

NAME:_____

ADDRESS_____

CITY_____ST_____ZIP_____

Card Type_____Card Number_____

Exp____/____ Signature _____

We accept VISA MASTERCARD AMERICAN EXPRESS & DISCOVER